ETERNAL SPIRIT OF THE CHAINLESS MIND

12 Themes in English Poetry

Oksun Kang ▪ Steven Reeder

Shinasa

ETERNAL SPIRIT OF THE CHAINLESS MIND
12 Themes in English Poetry

By

Oksun Kang ▪ Steven Reeder

SHINASA Publishing Co.
28-36 2F Nokbeon-Dong Eunpyung-Ku Seoul, Korea
Registered: 9-52 (January 5, 1956)
Tel: (02) 382-6411
Fax: (02) 382-6401
E-mail: shinasa@daum.net
Homepage: www.shinasa.co.kr

First published March, 2007
Second published February, 2015

Price: 정가 15,000원

ISBN: 978-89-8396-565-2

Contents

PART II PARALLELS

World Enough and Time:

A Prologue

Poetry is art. It is not singular in purpose, and as you will find out in this text, there are many different ways to look at the art of poetry. Like a good painting, you cannot merely just walk by with a passing glance. Sure, you may catch the overall outline of the scene painted masterfully on the canvas, but that is all you get—the outline. What of the colors? Light? Location of the objects? What angle and thickness did the artist apply the paint to create the illusion of life? Like all good works of art, poetry has subtexts and metaphors that operate on various levels. One could easily read the poem and then paraphrase what was read, but that is the outline. What of the words? Metaphors? The rhythm of the poem? What does the poet really mean and who is he or she really talking about? The answer to these questions opens our eyes and hearts to a greater world of creativity.

Thus, we, the editors, have selected twelve broad themes that most poetry has fallen into over the ages. Of our twelve themes, we have divided them into six parts—contrasts and parallels. The two parts were selected to show how different themes compliment each other. In contrast are the following themes: Love and War; Mythic and Visions of Everyday; Nature and Death. The paralleled themes are as follows: Personal

Identity and Solitude; Art and Concrete Poems; Freedom and Christian Themes. Of course many poems easily cross over into other themes, but we placed these poems into the context of their main message.

At the beginning of each chapter is an introduction to the theme and an overview of how the poems fit into the theme. It is important for students to read this, for it helps in the understanding of the poem and elicits ideas for further study. Following the poems is a section for difficult words and phrases encountered in the main texts. These words were selected on the basis of what we considered a student would probably go to the dictionary to look up. Most words included have multiple meanings or are archaic and may have different meanings than are used today. Please use this section to get the correct meaning. The final section is the study questions. These are included to get students thinking about the poems, to show how to analyze the poems, and also to help with essay topics. These are by far not the only questions to ask or think about, but they do try to encompass all the poems in relation to the topic.

It is the goal of the editors that this book will further interest in poetry. It is only an introduction and a selection of poems that we found as some of the most creative in the English language. We were also limited to poems from the public domain. This meant that they had to have been published before 1923. Unfortunately, this meant that many talented twentieth century poets could not be included in this volume. Their voices will be missed.

The next time you see a poem, we hope that you approach it as a great work of art, aware of all the intricate rhythm, rhyme, and metaphors layered throughout, and read it as something more than a curiosity; we hope you relish it as the key to the understanding of human nature, knowledge, and experience.

PART I

CONTRASTS

I. THEME ONE: LOVE

Introduction

Poetic Texts

Words & Phrases

Study Questions

INTRODUCTION TO THEME ONE

Love

Love, as a word, is difficult enough to comprehend let alone expound. It took the ancient Greek philosopher Plato seven lengthy dialogues to even try to come to an understanding of what love is. Our task in this chapter is a little less daunting and far simpler. We are going to tackle the idea of love with six simple poems by some of England's most respected poets.

Love is often ambiguous. And like love, a poet's tone is just as unclear. But what is not unclear are the intentions of all the male poets featured. We will look at the ideas expressed in Plato's *Symposium* (385 BCE) through just four characters: Pausianus, Aristophanes, Socrates, and the vulgar Alcibiades. First, Pausianus. An idea that is often found in male poetics is *carpe diem*, Latin for "seize the day!" In the Elizabethan time, *carpe diem* poetry was used as a way to remind the readers to live life to the fullest and not to waste love with coyness since time and youth are temporary. The phrase is a Classical idea that dates back to Roman times when the poet Horace (circa 65 B.C.-8 B.C.) wrote, "Seize the day, trust tomorrow as little as possible." *Carpe diem* fits with Pausianus' idea of love. He states that there are two kinds of love: vulgar and spiritual. Vulgar love is interested only in physical pleasure; whereas, spiritual love is concerned with both physical pleasure and, more importantly, loving the soul of a person.

First of our *carpe diem* poems is Ben Jonson's "Song: To

Celia," a more traditional variant of seizing the day. Here he uses memorable metaphors to sing praises of a woman's beauty. Jonson (1572-1637) was actually rephrasing famous lines from the *Epistles of Philostratus* written in the third century A.D. Compare Philostratus' *Letter XXIV*, "Drink to me with thine eyes only. Or, if thou wilt, putting the cup to thy lips, fill it with kisses, and so bestow it upon me," with the opening lines in Jonson's poem: "Drink to me, only with thine eyes / And I will pledge with mine; / Or leave a kiss but in the cup." There is a romantic quality to the verse and rhyme scheme that would make any woman swoon, which is exactly the role of *carpe diem* poetry. Modern critics would criticize this style of poetry as sentimental and singular in goal—to have a woman fall for the man—yet Jonson has avoided that with the easy flowing use of both assonance (Or leave a **k**iss but in the **c**up; **D**oth ask a **d**rink **d**ivine) and hyperbole (saying her kiss is greater than the nectar of the gods). Every word and stress flows beautifully into an unsung song that sends hearts aflutter. Notice, as well, that Jonson seems just as interested in the woman's soul as he is with her body.

The second *carpe diem* poem Andrew Marvell's "To His Coy Mistress" is opposite in nature. Where Jonson uses common English ideas that marry symbol and image, Marvell (1621-1678) takes a step further by writing paradox with grand, epic ideas that span the globe. He invokes images of his humble hometown river of Humber with the magical river Ganges in India (paradoxical). He speaks of loving her from the time of Noah—the mythological time that humanity started over—to the conversion of the Jews, which is supposed to take place at the end of the world according the "Book of Revelations" in the Bible. A comparison of images that Jonson used (cups, kisses, souls, gods, nectar, wreaths) with Marvell's (the Flood, conversion of the Jews, vegetable love, forehead, deserts, ashes, graves, pores, birds of prey, iron gates of life) shows that "To His Coy Mistress" uses imagery not normally related to love poetry (see also John Donne's "The Flea"). Marvell does exceed Jonson with the hyperbole, and his overuse of it only affirms the *carpe diem* idea that there is not a better time than now for love making. Remember that it is not the fact that the narrator isn't getting any love from his mistress, it is because he isn't getting enough. There lies the desperation and turns the poem from crass into romanticism.

John Donne's "The Flea" turns this idea on its head by going from romantic to crass. Donne (1572-1631) also shows us Aristophanes' argument as to why we need love. Aristophanes illustrates our pursuit of the opposite sex through a mythic tale of a time when people were round and composed of both male and female parts. When they challenged Zeus' authority, he cut them in half with a lightning bolt, causing both halves to search endlessly for the other. This explains why we feel empty without our better half. In "The Flea," the narrator, lying in bed with his love, has picked up a flea that has bitten him and then jumped over to her, probably landing on her breast, and has just bitten her. A common theory in Donne's day was that sexual relation was a mixing of a man's and woman's blood; therefore, he compares their love making to the mixing of their blood in the flea. If such a mixing of blood with a flea does not bother the woman, then how could their own love making? And since they have become "one flesh" in the flea, they are, practically speaking, married; thus, they have all legal and moral right to have sex. The maiden's prompt reply is to squish the flea with her finger. He claims this is similar to murder since both their blood resides in the flea. Because killing the flea and committing sacrilege was so simple, then it should be just as easy to give into his demands for love making. Here, *carpe diem* is at its most urgent with the full blessing of God, as is seen in all the religious imagery used, for to deny the narrator his need for love making is to commit heresy; she is denying the very primal urge to be whole again.

Another form of love poetry is the pastoral poem. Though the pastoral fits into three subjects—eclogue (singing contest), monologue, and elegy (lament for the dead)—the monologue is used for love poetry. The pastoral monologue often has a lovesick shepherd praising his love in high, courtly language fit more for the lordly manors than the rustic fields. This style of poetry is similar in nature to Socrates' idea of love, where spiritual love is the desire for beauty and not wholeness as Aristophanes states. Socrates teaches that spiritual love is the ultimate form but must be with someone who is moral and virtuous. Christopher Marlowe's (1564-1593) "The Passionate Shepherd" is similar to the pastoral genre as Jonson's "To Celia" is to *carpe diem*. The main difference between the two, though they both are pleading for the love of a woman, is that the pastoral invokes all the rustic images of farm life into the life of the lovers instead of the single beauty of the woman. *Carpe diem* poetry is all about the lover and lovemaking here and now; a pastoral is more relaxed and has a lifetime to enjoy the love. Marlowe's poem is also highly romantic in tone and rhythmic in form; it suggests a more innocent mind in crafting it.

Although the shepherd in Marlowe's pastoral never explicitly says the woman he is speaking of is a nymph, a Greek version of a fairy, Sir Walter Raleigh's (1552-1618) reply to this poem confirms it. In "The Nymph's Reply to the Shepherd," the nymph, an immortal being, rebukes the shepherd for his proposal by stating all the things he offers her will wither and die, as the shepherd and his love surely will. This pastoral is set in stark contrast to Marlowe's, suggesting such romanticism is childish and naïve. Marlowe's shepherd may think there is a lifetime of lovemaking, yet Raleigh's nymph suggests that such a lifetime isn't long enough, proposing an opposing idea to *carpe diem*, in that love is not a trifle thing to speak of idly but an eternal notion that mortals have yet to understand. This is similar to vulgar Alcibiades argument, which is the most reasonable, in that love is a two way street. Both the lover and the beloved must share mutual feelings for each other. This is the ingredient that is sorely lacking from most love poetry.

Finally, Sir Thomas Wyatt the Elder's (1503-1542) "Tangled I Was in Love's Snare" brings us to the very idea that love is a trap to escape from. The narrator, having fallen victim to the fairness of love, finds out first hand that it is nothing but "bitter woe." There is a sense that the narrator followed carnal desire over real love, for it was "her wily looks my wits did blind" that allows him to agree to follow her. Yet he comes to his senses before he marries her and gains his liberty as a bachelor once more and a lesson learned from the "labor lost," though a small gain it may have been. This is the lesson Socrates wanted us to learn when we fall in love with another over looks rather than moral virtue. What would seem to be love at first sight turns out to be infatuation. Love must be something we desire forever; thus, beauty must be coupled with a deeper intelligence where both male and female pursue a higher state of awareness more than vulgar "love-making."

Ben Jonson

Song: To Celia

Drink to me only with thine eyes,
        And I will pledge with mine;
Or leave a kiss but in the cup,
        And I'll not look for wine.
The thirst that from the soul doth rise,
        Doth ask a drink divine:
But might I of Jove's nectar sup,
        I would not change for thine.

I sent thee late a rosy wreath,
        Not so much honoring thee,
As giving it a hope, that there
        It could not withered be.
But thou thereon did'st only breathe,
        And sent'st it back to me;
Since when it grows and smells, I swear,
        Not of itself, but thee.

Andrew Marvell

To His Coy Mistress

Had we but world enough, and time,
This coyness, lady, were no crime.
We would sit down and think which way
To walk and pass our long love's day.
Thou by the Indian Ganges' side
Shouldst rubies find; I by the tide
Of Humber would complain. I would
Love you ten years before the Flood,
And you should, if you please, refuse
Till the conversion of the Jews.
My vegetable love should grow
Vaster than empires and more slow.
An hundred years should go to praise
Thine eyes and on thy forehead gaze,
Two hundred to adore each breast,
But thirty thousand to the rest,
An age at least to every part,
And the last age should show your heart.
For, lady, you deserve this state[1],
Nor would I love at lower rate.

But at my back I always hear
Time's wingèd chariot hurrying near,
And yonder all before us lie

---

1 high station in life

Deserts of vast eternity.
Thy beauty shall no more be found,
Nor, in thy marble vault, shall sound
My echoing song; then worms shall try
That long-preserved virginity,
And your quaint honor[2] turn to dust,
And into ashes all my lust.
The grave's a fine and private place,
But none, I think, do there embrace.

Now therefore, while the youthful hue
Sits on thy skin like morning dew,
And while thy willing soul transpires
At every pore with instant fires,
Now let us sport us while we may;
And now, like amorous birds of prey,
Rather at once our time devour
Than languish in his slow-chapped[3] power.
Let us roll all our strength and all
Our sweetness up into one ball;
And tear our pleasures with rough strife
Thorough the iron gates of life.
Thus, though we cannot make our sun
Stand still, yet we will make him run.

---

2 planned virtue

3 chewing slowly

John Donne

The Flea

Mark but this flea, and mark in this,
How little that which thou deny'st me is;
It sucked me first, and now sucks thee,
And in this flea our two bloods mingled be;
Thou know'st that this cannot be said
A sin, nor shame, nor loss of maidenhead,
    Yet this enjoys before it woo,
    And pampered swells with one blood made of two,
    And this, alas, is more than we would do.

Oh stay, three lives in one flea spare,
Where we almost, yea more then married are,
This flea is you and I, and this
Our marriage bed, and marriage temple is;
Though parents grudge, and you, we're met,
And cloistered in these living walls of jet.
    Though use[4] make you apt to kill me,
    Let not to that, self-murder added be,
    And sacrilege, three sins in killing three.

Cruel and sudden, hast thou since
Purpled thy nail, in blood of innocence?
Wherein could this flea guilty be,
Except in that drop it sucked from thee?

---

[4] custom

Yet thou triumph'st, and say'st that thou
Find'st not thyself, nor me, the weaker now;
　　'Tis true; then learn how false, fears be;
　　Just so much honor, when thou yield'st to me,
　　Will waste, as this flea's death took life from thee.

Christopher Marlowe

The Passionate Shepherd to His Love

Come live with me and be my love,
And we will all the pleasures prove,
That valleys, groves, hills, and fields,
Woods, or steepy mountain yields.

And we will sit upon the rocks,
Seeing the shepherds feed their flocks,
By shallow rivers, to whose falls
Melodious birds sing madrigals.

And I will make thee beds of roses
And a thousand fragrant posies,
A cap of flowers, and a kirtle
Embroidered all with leaves of myrtle;

A gown made of the finest wool
Which from our pretty lambs we pull;
Fair lined slippers for the cold,
With buckles of the purest gold;

A belt of straw and ivy buds,
With coral clasps and amber studs;
And if these pleasures may thee move,
Come live with me, and be my love.

The shepherds' swains shall dance and sing

For thy delight each May morning:
If these delights thy mind may move,
Then live with me and be my love.

Sir Walter Raleigh

The Nymph's Reply to the Shepherd

A response to Marlowe's "Passionate Shepherd"

If all the world and love were young,
And truth in every shepherd's tongue,
These pretty pleasures might me move
To live with thee and be thy love.

Time drives the flocks from field to fold
When rivers rage and rocks grow cold,
And Philomel becometh dumb;
The rest complains of cares to come.

The flowers do fade, and wanton fields
To wayward winter reckoning yields;
A honey tongue, a heart of gall,
Is fancy's spring, but sorrow's fall,

The gowns, thy shoes, thy beds of roses,
Thy cap, thy kirtle, and thy posies
Soon break, soon wither, soon forgotten--
In folly ripe, in reason rotten.

Thy belt of straw and ivy buds,
Thy coral clasps and somber studs,
All these in me no means can move
To come to thee and be thy love.

But could youth last and love still breed,
Had joys no date nor age no need,
Then these delights my mind might move
To live with thee and be thy love.

Sir Thomas Wyatt the Elder

Tangled I Was in Love's Snare

Tangled I was in love's snare,
Oppressed with pain, torment with care,
Of grief right sure, of joy full bare,
Clean in despair by cruelty,
But ha! ha! ha! full well is me,
For I am now at liberty.

The woeful day so full of pain,
The weary night all spent in vain,
The labor lost for so small gain,
To write them all it will not be.
But ha! ha! ha! full well is me,
For I am now at liberty.

Everything that fair doth show,
When proof is made it proveth not so,
But turneth mirth to bitter woe;
Which in this case full well I see.
But ha! ha! ha! full well is me,
For I am now at liberty.

Too great desire was my guide,
And wanton[5] will went by my side;
Hope ruléd still, and made me bide

---

[5] sexually unrestrained

Of love's craft th' extremity.
But ha! ha! ha! full well is me,
For I am now at liberty.

With feignéd words that were but wind,
To long delays I was assigned;
Her wily looks my wits did blind;
Thus as she would I did agree.
But ha! ha! ha! full well is me,
For I am now at liberty.

Was never bird tangled in lime
That brake away in better time
Than I, that rotten boughs did climb,
And had no hurt, but 'scapéd[6] free.
Now ha! ha! ha! full well is me,
For I am now at liberty.

---

6 escaped

Words & Phrases

amorous: (adj) showing love.
apt: (adj) inclined.
bide: (v) old form of endure.
cloister: (v) to confine, especially in a monastery.
coy: (adj) shy or modest.
doth: (v) old form of does.
feigned: (adj) disguised.
Flood, the: (n) the great Biblical Flood in the time of Noah.
Ganges: (n) a major river flowing out of the Himalayas into India. It is considered sacred.
hue: (n) color.
Humber: (n) a small river in Trent, England.
Jove: (n) Roman for Jupiter. The Greek name is Zeus.
kirtle: (n) skirt.
lime: (n) birdlime; a sticky substance smeared on trees to catch small birds.
madrigal: (n) a harmonic song.
maidenhead: (n) virginity.
mirth: (n) joy.
myrtle: (n) a shrub.
pampered: (adj) old form meaning to eat a lot.
Philomel: (n) the nightingale.
posies: (n) a bouquet of flowers
prey: (n) an animal hunted by another animal.
quaint: (adj) old fashioned charm.
'st: old form to mark 2nd person singular.
strife: (n) a struggle.
sup: (v) to eat supper.

swain: (n) lover
thee: (prn) old form of you.
thine: (prn) old form of yours.
thorough: (adj) old form of through.
thy: (prn) old form of your.
tis: a contraction of it is.
transpire: (v) old form of breathe.
wanton: (adj) full of vegetation.
woe: (n) sadness.
woo: (v) to attract the love of another.
yea: (adv) old form of indeed.
yield: (v) to surrender one's power over to another.
yonder: (adj) over there.

Study Questions

1. A couplet contains two lines in a poem that usually rhyme. All the poems in this section are couplet poems, usually having a rhyme scheme of *aa, bb, cc, dd* and so on. All the featured poets in this section were of the Elizabethan Era, which found favor with the couplet as the ultimate form of rhyme. Which couplet poem do you like best? Why?

2. Which couplet love poem do you find more effective? Why?

3. Reread Jonson, Marvel, and Donne's poems. Remember that these are *carpe diem* love poems. What is your opinion of *carpe diem* love poems? Do they have much merit in modern times?

4. Which is your favorite *carpe diem* love poem? Explain.

5. Reread Donne's "The Flea." What is the narrator talking about? What role does the flea play for the narrator in stanzas one and three? What role does the flea play in the second stanza? Why does the narrator use a flea as an example to speak about?

6. Reread Marvel's "To His Coy Mistress." What is the narrator talking about here? Is his goal the same or different than the narrator's goal in "The Flea"? Should these poems be considered "anti-feminist" poems? Why or why not? How should a woman react to such poems?

7. Do you think the women in either Marvel or Donne's poems will do what they are asked to do? Why or why not? Give details from the poems to support your answer.

8. Reread Marlowe's "The Passionate Shepherd to His Love." How is it similar to Donne and Marvel's poems? How is it different?

9. Of all these poems, who do you think is being serious? Who do you think is being sarcastic? Explain both your answers with examples from the poems.

10. Write a list of lines or phrases from each poem that best portrays the *carpe diem* viewpoint.

11. Would you use any of these poems to give to your lover? Why or why not? If you would choose one, which one would you choose? Explain.

12. Sir Walter Raleigh's poem "The Nymph's Reply to the Shepherd" is in response to the themes expressed in Marlowe's poem. How are these two poems different?

13. What themes does Marlowe's poem express? What themes does Raleigh's poem express? Who is more correct in his ideas? Explain.

14. Who wrote the better poem?

15. Hyperbole is poetic exaggeration. Which poem uses

hyperbole to the extreme? Use examples from the poem to support your answer.

II. THEME TWO: **WAR**

Introduction

Poetic Texts

Words & Phrases

Study Questions

INTRODUCTION OF THEME TWO

War

If love is such a noble state that should be desired, then why is there so much hate? Opposition in all things shows us that one cannot know the light without there being darkness; we cannot know the good without the bad; and we cannot know love without war. Seven poets from both sides of the Atlantic paint us two separate pictures of war and its effects upon humanity. For the sake of this chapter, if we can simplify love as a celebration of humanity, then war can also be simplified here as an outward hatred towards those whom we refuse to understand.

The first type of war is over religion, where one group refuses to accept the other. Running counter to any religious idea of tolerance and love, holy wars are a stain upon any religious history. Our first poet, John Milton (1608-1674), wrote of his indignation, as well as other Protestants' throughout England and Europe, toward the Catholic slaughter of the Waldensians in 1655. The Waldensians were founded around 1173 and were considered heretics by the Catholic Church. By the twelfth century, they were offered Piedmont, a region in northern Italy, to be a place of safety from Catholic persecution. Though it angered the Pope at the time (referred to as the triple tyrant in the poem), they lived in peace. By the Reformation in the sixteenth century, they were thought to be safe from any persecution. With the head of the Catholic Church in Rome, having a whole region of "heretics" in the same country was shameful to many. Eventually, the persecution turned to an all out massacre as the region was purged of any dissenter. Survivors fled to the Alps and into Switzerland, being chased all the way. Large groups of stragglers were trapped in caves and suffocated as huge fires were built at the entrance with the smoke fanned inside. The women and children who survived the initial purge were also hounded in the mountains, and, when caught, both mother and child were thrown off the cliffs.

Stephen Crane (1871-1900) offers his thoughts on the very same idea of senseless war. No matter how "just" or "holy" the war may seem both Milton and Crane show that it is the women and the children who suffer the most. Crane's poem is timeless in the sense that it can be narrated at any time in history during any theater of war; it applies to the senselessness that war is created from. With such death and destruction, it leads the narrator of Crane's poem to question why. Ironically, Crane never answers the question, for it is one that millions still struggle to answer everyday.

Though some wars are fought in the name of religion, it is, in fact, religion that helps many deal with the horrors of war. Wilfred Owen (1893-1918) found his poetic voice in the harsh trenches of World War I. Deeply religious, Owen infused his own poetry with Biblical images and themes of sacrifice and Hell. Owen was teaching privately in Bordeaux, France when war broke out, and he visited a hospital full of wounded soldiers. At that moment, he decided to return to England and enlist. He thought he could both lead his countrymen in battle and inspire them with words. He fought trench warfare in France where he was injured several times. He wrote most of his poetry in the hospital between 1917 and 1918. Having seen the horror of war first hand and experienced it himself, his poetry is marked by irony where he attacked those who favored war as he condemned the war itself. His "Anthem for Doomed Youth," a lament for those needlessly sacrificed in the war, would also be his own epitaph. By June 1918, he had fully recovered and was sent back to France. He fought bravely but was killed a full week before the Armistice that ended the war on November 11, 1918. His parents received the notification of his death on the same day as the Armistice. "No mockeries now for them; no prayers nor bells; / Nor any voice of mourning save the choirs, / The shrill, demented choirs of wailing shells; / And bugles calling for them from sad shires."

So why? Why do we fight wars? Rupert Brooke (1887-1915) tells us in his poem "The Soldier" that we do so out of patriotism, love for our country. In this light, perhaps war and love are not as contrasting as we first thought. "If I should die, think only this of me: / That there's some corner of a foreign field / That is for ever England." Brooke was a "pro" war poet, writing poems of inspiration at the outbreak of World War I. To show his own patriotism, he enlisted in the British Navy. He didn't see much fighting but was wounded, and died a year later from blood poisoning coming from that same wound. Though his words were highly optimistic, war claimed him, as it claimed his "Soldier," an honor for anyone who wishes to preserve their way of life in the land of their fathers.

Walt Whitman (1819-1892) gives us a wonderful sketch of the heroic quality of soldiers in his "Calvary Crossing a Ford" written during the American Civil War (1861-1865). Though we are not told which side they are fighting for, or who any individual soldier is, we are given an almost "god-like" description of these men who are fighting for a greater goal than themselves. As a compliment to this image we have A.E. Housman's (1859-1936) World War I poem "Epitaph on an Army of Mercenaries," which was written after the first battle Ypres, in southwest Belgium. There the British were able to stop the Germans from approaching the English Channel in 1914 at a great cost of lives. His direct and efficient verse is able to conjure images of doom to stir pity for those who were brave enough to fight for "what God abandoned."

Finally, Lord Alfred Tennyson's (1809-1892) poem "Charge of the Light Brigade" may answer our question best of why we fight war when he writes, "Theirs not to reason why / Theirs but to do and die;" thus, showing the heroic bravery of soldiers in warfare though their fate is doomed to die. The poem actually memorializes a charge that occurred in the Battle of Balaclava on October 25, 1854 during the Crimean War fought between Russia on one side and France, United Kingdom, and the Ottoman Empire on the other. The British Light Brigade received orders to charge down into a valley guarded by both artillery and riflemen in an effort to stop a shipment line of weapons to the Russians. Though the charge was bold and heroic, it failed at great loss of life with 118 killed, 127 wounded, and 362 horses lost. The outcome may have failed, but it placed the British calvery in high regard for bravery and ferociousness. No matter why war is fought, death, destruction, and suffering being as much a part of life as war, it would seem only justifiable if it were fought out of love: love for country, love for humanity, and love for freedom.

John Milton

On the Late Massacre in Piedmont

Avenge, O Lord, thy slaughtered saints, whose bones
Lie scattered on the Alpine mountains cold,
Even them who kept thy truth so pure of old
When all our fathers worshiped stocks and stones;
Forget not: in thy book[1] record their groans
Who were thy sheep and in their ancient fold
Slain by the bloody Piedmontese that rolled
Mother with infant down the rocks. Their moans
The vales redoubled to the hills, and they
To Heaven. Their martyred blood and ashes sow
O'er all th' Italian fields where still doth sway
The triple tyrant[2]; that from these may grow
A hundred-fold, who having learnt thy way
Early may fly the Babylonian woe.

---

1 The Book of Life

2 The Pope who wears a triple crown on his Papal Tiara no longer worn today

Stephen Crane

There Was Crimson Clash of War

There was crimson clash of war.
Lands turned black and bare;
Women wept;
Babes ran, wondering.
There came one who understood not these things.
He said, "Why is this?"
Whereupon a million strove to answer him.
There was such intricate clamor of tongues,
That still the reason was not.

Wilfred Owen

Anthem for Doomed Youth

What passing-bells for these who die as cattle?
        Only the monstrous anger of the guns.
        Only the stuttering rifles' rapid rattle
Can patter out their hasty orisons.
No mockeries now for them; no prayers nor bells;
        Nor any voice of mourning save the choirs—
The shrill, demented choirs of wailing shells;
        And bugles calling for them from sad shires.

What candles may be held to speed them all?
        Not in the hands of boys, but in their eyes
Shall shine the holy glimmers of good-byes.
        The pallor of girls' brows shall be their pall;
Their flowers the tenderness of patient minds,
And each slow dusk a drawing-down of blinds.

Rupert Brooke

The Soldier

If I should die, think only this of me:
That there's some corner of a foreign field
That is for ever England. There shall be
In that rich earth a richer dust concealed;
A dust whom England bore, shaped, made aware,
Gave, once, her flowers to love, her ways to roam,
A body of England's, breathing English air,
Washed by the rivers, blest by suns of home.

And think, this heart, all evil shed away,
A pulse in the eternal mind, no less
Gives somewhere back the thoughts by England given;
Her sights and sounds; dreams happy as her day;
And laughter, learnt of friends; and gentleness,
In hearts at peace, under an English heaven.

Walt Whitman

Cavalry Crossing a Ford

A line in long array where they wind betwixt green islands,
They take a serpentine course, their arms flash in the sun--hark to the musical clank,
Behold the silvery river, in it the splashing horses loitering stop to drink,
Behold the brown-faced men, each group, each person a picture, the negligent rest on the saddles,
Some emerge on the opposite bank, others are just entering the ford--while,
Scarlet and blue and snowy white,
The guidon flags flutter gaily in the wind.

A. E. Housman

Epitaph on an Army of Mercenaries

These, in the day when heaven was falling,
The hour when earth's foundations fled,
Follow'd their mercenary calling
And took their wages and are dead.

Their shoulders held the sky suspended;
They stood, and earth's foundations stay;
What God abandon'd, these defended,
And saved the sum of things for pay

Alfred, Lord Tennyson

The Charge of the Light Brigade

Half a league half a league,
Half a league onward,
All in the valley of Death
Rode the six hundred:
"Forward, the Light Brigade!
Charge for the guns" he said:
Into the valley of Death
Rode the six hundred.

"Forward, the Light Brigade!"
Was there a man dismayed?
Not tho' the soldier knew
Some one had blundered:
Theirs not to make reply,
Theirs not to reason why,
Theirs but to do & die,
Into the valley of Death
Rode the six hundred.

Cannon to right of them,
Cannon to left of them,
Cannon in front of them
Volleyed & thundered;
Stormed at with shot and shell,
Boldly they rode and well,
Into the jaws of Death,

Into the mouth of Hell
Rode the six hundred.

Flashed all their sabers bare,
Flashed as they turned in air
Sabering the gunners there,
Charging an army while
All the world wondered:
Plunged in the battery-smoke
Right thro' the line they broke;
Cossack & Russian
Reeled from the saber-stroke,
Shattered & sundered.
Then they rode back, but not
Not the six hundred.

Cannon to right of them,
Cannon to left of them,
Cannon behind them
Volleyed and thundered;
Stormed at with shot and shell,
While horse & hero fell,
They that had fought so well
Came thro' the jaws of Death,
Back from the mouth of Hell,
All that was left of them,
Left of six hundred.

When can their glory fade?
O the wild charge they made!

All the world wondered.
Honor the charge they made!
Honor the Light Brigade,
Noble six hundred!

Words & Phrases

battery: (n) a combined group of artillery, like cannons.
betwixt: (prep) between.
brigade: (n) a large group of military troops.
clamor of tongues: babble; so many talking nothing is understood.
Cossack: (n) A southern Russian horseman.
ford: (n) a place where the water is shallow enough to cross.
guidon: (n) a small military flag that identifies a unit.
loiter: (v) to wait around idly.
negligent: (adj) careless.
orison: (n) a prayer.
pall: (n) coffin.
pallor: (n) very pale or white.
Piedmontese: (n) the Waldensians who lived in Piedmont, Italy.
redouble: (v) echo.
saber: (n) a slightly curved sword used by cavalry.
shire: (n) a British county.
stock: (n) wood; especially a wooden idol in this poem.
strove: (v) past tense of strive; to try hard.
sunder: (v) to divide into two parts.

Study Questions

1. A.E. Housman (1859-1936) is said to have influenced later generations of poets with his poetry. He was able to bridge the gap between the poetry of the past with the poetry of the present with simplistic language; "Epitaph on an Army of Mercenaries" is a good example of this. How does this new technique of simplicity compare to the usual heightened language found in poets of the past? Does such simplicity lend itself to such a dreary poem? Would you say this is a negative poem or is it positive? Explain.

2. The "war poets" in this anthology are Rupert Brooke and Wilfred Owen; war claimed both of them. Again look at their language compared with Housman's. What is the style of their language? Why do they write this way? What do you notice they are trying to say with their poems? Are they for or against the war? What evidence is there for you conclusion?

3. Which poem about war do you like the best? Why? Do they make war any more real for you? Why or why not?

4. Reread Walt Whitman's and Lord Tennyson's poems. Now compare the tone of their poems with the tone of the war poets. Are they similar or different? Explain. What does this say about 20th century poetry before the end of World War I?

5. According to any of these poems, can war ever be justified? Why or why not? Use examples from the poem(s).

6. Tennyson wrote his poem ten years after the Crimean War. The situation was similar to the current war in Iraq; most of the British people did not want to participate in either war. Tennyson wrote the poem to stir patriotism in the hearts of the people. Do you think this poem works to stir patriotism and favor for an unfavorable war? Explain. Do you think this poem would work to bolster favor for today's war? Why or why not?

7. Which war poem resonates the most emotionally? Which one makes you feel for what the poet is saying? Explain.

8. Milton's poem is of the suffering of innocents under war and especially of full scale slaughter. Remember it was the slaughter of a "heretical" sect by the Catholic Church, which was the current ruling institution in Europe. Is there a parallel with then and now? Could the suffering and killing of the Waldensians be paralleled to the suffering and killing of Muslims today? Explain.

9. Reread Tennyson's "The Charge of the Light Brigade." Note the meter used throughout the poem. It uses two stressed syllables, dimeter, followed by two unstressed syllables, dactyl. The first foot of each meter is stressed and then falls always making use of falling rhythm. Why would Tennyson use this form in his poem? Read the poem out loud to hear and feel the falling rhythm and then imagine the scene it creates for you. What oral image is he trying to create?

III. THEME THREE: MYTHIC THEMES

Introduction

Poetic Texts

Words & Phrases

Study Questions

INTRODUCTION TO THEME THREE

Mythic Themes

What separates a mythic tale from everyday life is the use of the supernatural in order to understand natural experiences. Bringing human ideas into a cosmic reality gives insubstantial ideas tangible form. There are no inconsistencies when we read myth; everything and anything is possible within that certain realm. Myth also allows us to view various social and political patterns that exist or have existed through numerous cultures, and the older the myth lasted, the more cultures it encompassed. Thus, myth invoked through poetry taps into the collective idea of the world in order to bring understanding to abstract ideas that may not be understood through the mundane.

A good example of setting abstract ideas into concrete images is Samuel Taylor Coleridge's (1772-1834) "Kubla Khan." How would you write about your own failure to complete what could possibly be the greatest achievement of your entire career? For many, this would be an impossible feat. For Coleridge, he used the mythic appeal of the historical city Xanadu, which was the summer palace of real life Mongol emperor Kublai Khan (1215-1294; grandson of Genghis Khan), as a metaphor for the exotic creativity of unsurpassed individuals. The poem is broken up into four parts. The first three are his attempt to capture the magnificence of Kubla Khan's pleasure palace that Coleridge had read about before he entered a drug induced sleep. In his dream, he envisioned writing around 300 lines of the most exquisite poetry in honor of this ancient emperor's endeavor. In his mind's eye, he had already written the very words that his subconscious had conjured; he could grasp it as if he were actually present. It was wondrous to behold! Then he awoke and set to pen the very writing he had envisioned. He wrote as he never had before; the poem, in its entirety, would be his greatest masterpiece. After the first three stanzas were set to his satisfaction, a knock came to the door, and a certain man with unexplained business distracted Coleridge from his task for about an hour. When the poet sat down again to finish his eager symphony of words, he was at a loss. The vision was gone! The fourth stanza is but a remorseful reminder of his attempt to invoke the muse (the "damsel with a dulcimer") to return his grand vision. "Could I revive within me / her symphony and song, / To such a deep delight 'twould win me, / That with music loud and long, / I would build that dome in air." Thus he ended his poem of grand design with a plea and knew he could go no further. He had been to the edge of paradise and forgotten what it was like! "For he on honey-dew hath fed, / And drunk the milk of paradise."

Myth also inspires feelings of awe that often brings about certain understandings called epiphany, an enlightening revelation. For John Keats (1795-1821), who had already read Homer's *Iliad* and *Odyssey* translated into free verse form or dry heroic couplets, an epiphany struck when he encountered the Elizabethan playwright George Chapman's translation of Homer's epics in lively verse. This was at a time when only the original language of such poetry was considered meaningful and translations were but boorish attempts at art. Impressed with classical themes and images, Keats sat down and penned his own response to Chapman's translations in his own heroic verse. Again, how does do you shout out to the world such an epiphany as finding poetic creativity of classical ideas in the vulgar English language? You respond in kind. Keats explores his emotions outside the everyday usage and moves into the mythic to show the reader just what it is like to experience the divine in words. The first half of the poem is an attempt to express his appreciation for all "the realms of gold" that he has read and that he has read a lot. Out of all that he has read, Homer is considered one of the finest story tellers, but not until Keats has experienced Chapman's translation, has he ever felt such elation. Keats recalls the discovery of Neptune, the "new planet," and how this changed the field of science at his time, and still his discovery of Chapman's Homer cannot even begin to compare with the elations of that. He talks of the emotions Spanish Cortez and his men must have felt when they reached the Pacific Ocean—although Keats is mistaken for it was actually another explorer. Keats' historical mistake is forgiven in context of his mythmaking. He is like a man discovering God for the first time. Oh, the rapture!

Continuing with the theme of Homer's *Iliad* and *Odyssey* is Lord Alfred Tennyson's "Ulysses," the Latin form of Odysseus. Here Tennyson continues the myth of Ulysses after his adventure in the Trojan War and his ten years of misadventures just to return to his wife and child, Telemachus. Ulysses, an antihero, is often a proud king and warrior, willing to sacrifice the men who follow him in pursuit of some ideal. In this poem, Tennyson attempts to capture the feeling of restlessness that one may feel after a lifetime of adventuring. The challenge is to put into words the feelings of an aged man who has walked with gods and defied them, outwitted giants, and heard the forlorn song of the sirens and lived. He is a man who would rather die in battle than of old age; he will leave his kingdom to his son and continue on adventuring. Ulysses is a tragic hero in the sense that, like Hercules, he has outsmarted the fates and survived the wrath of gods, yet he cannot escape his fate to die an old man. The disappointment that must accompany one after such a Herculean life only to find that mortality will eventually rob one of the glory and honor one has spent a lifetime acquiring. This is the epiphany; this is the tragedy. “One equal temper of heroic hearts, / Made weak by time and fate, but strong in will / To strive, to seek, to find, and not to yield.”

Helen Doolittle (H.D.; 1886-1961) has even found myth appealing for feminist criticism in her poem “Helen.” Helen, who was abducted by Paris of Troy that brought about the Trojan War when her Greek lover Menelaus took his armada to reclaim her, is the daughter of Zeus and mortal Leda. This is also the very same war that Ulysses went to fight in. In this poem, H.D. reminds the reader of how a male’s perspective of women is focused only upon beauty. H.D. tells us that “All Greece hates / the still eyes in the white face, / the luster of olives / where she stands, and the white hands.” She is hated, for many stories relate that Helen willingly left with Paris, betraying Greece for Troy. Yet if she is hated so, why is she described with such beauty? Even Menelaus, after the death of Paris and the capture of Helen, failed to slay her as promised; for as he raised his sword to strike her down, her beauty overwhelmed him so that he took her back to Greece. Greece has continuously disdained her for causing such a bloody conflict and so easily betraying her prince. However anyone feels of Helen, she is both legendary and beautiful, for she was born out of love Zeus held for Leda, and her own love, as powerful and misplaced as Zeus', resulted in much bloodshed. For this, H.D. shows in the second stanza what happens to women who are hated for being all too human—they turn to stone. There is a sense of Helen's beauty bleeding into colorless marble and the idea that history tries to ignore the woman and worship the beauty; death to the woman and a rebirth of a male's ideal of what a woman should be: lifeless beauty.

Even William Wordsworth (1770-1850), who found the simplicity of nature to be the most beautiful of things, used myth as a way to make sense of his own feelings towards materialism. In "The World Is Too Much with Us," Wordsworth sees too many people, even in 1807, "getting and spending" and losing touch with nature, which has the power to lift hearts and enrich souls. Wordsworth shifts to myth to illustrate how even "a Pagan suckled in a creed unknown" had created his own culture out of his own respect for nature. Think about this, what do you feel when you look upon the ocean or hear the wind blow, or even see a field of flowers? Nothing? Do you even allow yourself time to ponder such sights? Or are your eyes fixed to your cell phones, your ears locked to headphones, your hearts wrapped around riches and excess? So Wordsworth wails out his contempt and wishes he were a pagan of old worshipping nature instead of money, for what do you see when you look down the city street, or glance upon your bank book? When Wordsworth and other lovers of nature look upon the sea, they can see Proteus, the son of Poseidon, rising from the foam and hear Triton, another son, blowing his twisted conch shell to calm the waves of their rising. "Little we see in Nature that is ours; / We have given our hearts away, a sordid boon!" Materialism has little to offer but temporary goods; nature, on the other hand, offers a treasury of ideals, enough to sustain hundreds of cultures through thousands of years.

Our final myth, "Ozymandias" by Percy Bysshe Shelley (1792-1822), deals with the actual Egyptian pharaoh Ramesses II. Ozymandias is the Greek name for Ramesses. For Shelley, the idea of arrogance common with tyrannical leaders was almost laughable. The poem was written three years after Napoleon Bonaparte's crushing defeat at Waterloo and the demise of the French Empire; what started out as a revolution from tyranny (the French Revolution) that many in England supported, turned into tyranny and oppression again when Napoleon declared himself Emperor. Many, including Shelley, became disenfranchised by the hope that such a revolution could ever happen in England. In "Ozymandias," Shelley shows that the mighty pharaoh's own efforts to remain immortal throughout history are futile, and Napoleon's efforts, like Ozymandias, will soon end as "a shattered visage." Though this has not proved the case, for Shelley the idea of the myth, in fact, outlives the reality of a person. Ozymandias, perhaps Egypt's greatest pharaoh, whose only surviving legacy is a fallen statue with an inscription, according to Shelly, saying, "My name is Ozymandias, king of kings: / Look on my works, ye Mighty, and despair!" What is ironical is that nothing remains of his works. The only thing to despair is the fallen condition of his monument, which has nothing to do with the skill of a mighty pharaoh, but the craft of a lowly sculptor. Art exceeds ambition, as this poem also testifies.

Samuel Taylor Coleridge

Kubla Khan

In Xanadu did Kubla Khan
A stately pleasure-dome decree:
Where Alph, the sacred river, ran
Through caverns measureless to man
        Down to a sunless sea.
So twice five miles of fertile ground
With walls and towers were girdled round:
And there were gardens bright with sinuous rills,
Where blossomed many an incense-bearing tree;
And here were forests ancient as the hills,
Enfolding sunny spots of greenery.

But oh! that deep romantic chasm which slanted
Down the green hill athwart a cedarn cover!
A savage place! as holy and enchanted
As e'er beneath a waning moon was haunted
By woman wailing for her demon-lover!
And from this chasm, with ceaseless turmoil seething,
As if this earth in fast thick pants were breathing,
A mighty fountain momently was forced:
Amid whose swift half-intermitted burst
Huge fragments vaulted like rebounding hail,
Or chaffy grain beneath the thresher's flail:
And 'mid these dancing rocks at once and ever
It flung up momently the sacred river.
Five miles meandering with a mazy motion

Through wood and dale the sacred river ran,
Then reached the caverns measureless to man,
And sank in tumult to a lifeless ocean:
And 'mid this tumult Kubla heard from far
Ancestral voices prophesying war!
    The shadow of the dome of pleasure
    Floated midway on the waves;
    Where was heard the mingled measure
    From the fountain and the caves.
It was a miracle of rare device,
A sunny pleasure dome with caves of ice!

    A damsel with a dulcimer
    In a vision once I saw:
    It was an Abyssinian maid,
    And on her dulcimer she played,
    Singing of Mount Abora.
    Could I revive within me
    Her symphony and song,
    To such a deep delight 'twould win me,
That with music loud and long,
I would build that dome in air,
That sunny dome! those caves of ice!
And all who heard should see them there,
And all should cry, Beware! Beware!
His flashing eyes, his floating hair!
Weave a circle round him thrice,
And close your eyes with holy dread,
For he on honey-dew hath fed,
And drunk the milk of Paradise.

John Keats

On First Looking into Chapman's Homer

Much have I traveled in the realms of gold-
　　And many great states and kingdoms seen;
　　Round many western islands have I been
Which bards in fealty to Apollo have to hold.
Oft of one wide expanse had I been told
　　That deep-brow'd Homer ruled as his demesne;
　　Yet did I never breathe its pure serene
Till I heard Chapman shout out loud and bold!
Then felt I like a watcher of the skies,
　　When a new planet[1] swims into his ken;
Or like stout Cortez[2] when with eagle eyes when
　　He stared at the Pacific – and all of his men
Looked at each other with a wild surprise–
　　Silent - upon a peak in Darien.

---

1 The planet Neptune

2 Cortez, a Spanish explorer was not the first to see the Pacific. It was actually another less famous Spanish explorer Balboa.

Alfred, Lord Tennyson

Ulysses

It little profits that an idle king,
By this still hearth, among these barren crags,
Matched with an agèd wife, I mete and dole
Unequal laws unto a savage race,
That hoard, and sleep, and feed, and know not me.
I cannot rest from travel, I will drink
Life to the lees. All times I have enjoyed
Greatly, have suffered greatly, both with those
That loved me, and alone; on shore, and when
Through scudding drifts the rainy Hyades
Vexed the dim sea. I am become a name;
For always roaming with a hungry heart
Much have I seen and known,— cities of men
And manners, climates, councils, governments,
Myself not least, but honored of them all,—
And drunk delight of battle with my peers;
Far on the ringing plains of windy Troy.
I am part of all that I have met;
Yet all experience is an arch where through
Gleams that untravelled world whose margin fades
For ever and for ever when I move.
How dull it is to pause, to make an end,
To rust unburnished, not to shine in use!
As though to breathe were life! Life piled on life
Were all too little, and of one to me
Little remains, but every hour is saved

From that eternal silence, something more,
A bringer of new things; and vile it were
For some three suns to store and hoard myself,
And this gray spirit yearning in desire
To follow knowledge like a sinking star,
Beyond the utmost bound of human thought.
This is my son, mine own Telemachus,
To whom I leave the scepter and the isle,--
Well-loved of me, discerning to fulfill
This labor, by slow prudence to make mild
A rugged people, and through soft degrees
Subdue them to the useful and the good.
Most blameless is he, centered in the sphere
Of common duties, decent not to fail
In offices of tenderness, and pay
Meet adoration to my household gods,
When I am gone. He works his work, I mine.
There lies the port; the vessel puffs her sail;
There gloom the dark, broad seas. My mariners,
Souls that have toiled, and wrought, and thought with me,--
That ever with a frolic welcome took
The thunder and the sunshine, and opposed
Free hearts, free foreheads,--you and I are old;
Old age hath yet his honor and his toil.
Death closes all; but something ere the end,
Some work of noble note, may yet be done,
Not unbecoming men that strove with Gods.
The lights begin to twinkle from the rocks;
The long day wanes; the slow moon climbs; the deep

Moans round with many voices. Come, friends,
'Tis not too late to seek a newer world.
Push off, and sitting well in order smite
The sounding furrows; for my purpose holds
To sail beyond the sunset, and the baths
Of all the western stars, until I die.
It may be that the gulfs will wash us down;
It may be we shall touch the Happy Isles,
And see the great Achilles, whom we knew.
Though much is taken, much abides; and though
We are not now that strength which in old days
Moved earth and heaven; that which we are, we are;--
One equal temper of heroic hearts,
Made weak by time and fate, but strong in will
To strive, to seek, to find, and not to yield.

Hilda Doolittle

Helen

All Greece hates
the still eyes in the white face,
the luster as of olives
where she stands,
And the white hands.
All Greece reviles
the wan face when she smiles,
hating it deeper still
when it grows wan and white,
remembering past enchantments
And past ills.

Greece sees unmoved,
God's daughter, born of love,
the beauty of cool feet
and slenderest knees,
could love indeed the maid,
only if she were laid,
white ash amid funereal cypresses.

William Wordsworth

The World Is Too Much with Us

The world is too much with us; late and soon,
Getting and spending, we lay waste our powers;
Little we see in Nature that is ours;
We have given our hearts away, a sordid boon!
This Sea that bares her bosom to the moon,
The winds that will be howling at all hours,
And are up-gathered now like sleeping flowers,
For this, for everything, we are out of tune;
It moves us not.--Great God! I'd rather be
A Pagan suckled in a creed outworn;
So might I, standing on this pleasant lea,
Have glimpses that would make me less forlorn;
Have sight of Proteus rising from the sea;
Or hear old Triton blow his wreathèd horn.

Percy Bysshe Shelley

Ozymandias

I met a traveler from an antique land
Who said: "Two vast and trunkless legs of stone
Stand in the desert... Near them, on the sand,
Half sunk, a shattered visage lies, whose frown,
And wrinkled lip, and sneer of cold command,
Tell that its sculptor well those passions read
Which yet survive, stamped on these lifeless things,
The hand that mocked them and the heart that fed:
And on the pedestal these words appear:
'My name is Ozymandias, king of kings:
Look on my works, ye Mighty, and despair!'
Nothing beside remains. Round the decay
Of that colossal wreck, boundless and bare
The lone and level sands stretch far away"

Words & Phrases

abide: (v) remain.
Abyssinian: (adj) Ethiopian (former name).
Achilles: (n) the hero of Homer's Iliad.
Alph: (n) a mythological underground river that symbolizes secret knowledge.
Apollo: (n) the Greek and Roman god of poetry.
athwart: (adv) crosswise.
bard: (n) a poet.
boon: (n) treasure.
cedarn: (adj) looking like it was made of cedar or wood.
chasm: (n) see "fissure."
cypress: (n) a tree with dark green leaves.
Darien: (n) a mountain in eastern Panama, Central America
decree: (n) an order from a person in authority.
demesne: (n) a district or region.
device: (n) plan.
dole: (v) to give out sparingly.
dulcimer: (n) a stringed musical instrument
e'er: (adv) poetic form of ever.
ere: (prep) before.
fissure: (n) a large, deep yawning cut in a mountain.
frolic: (adj) cheerful.
girdled: (v) to encircle.
half-intermitted: (v) to be almost stopped.
Homer: (n) 9th century B.C. Greek poet of the *Iliad* and *Odyssey*
Hyades: (n) a cluster of stars.

ken: (n) knowledge.

lea: (n) a meadow.

lee: (n) a protective shelter.

luster: (n) shiny quality.

mazy: (adj) confusing turns like a maze.

mete: (v) to distribute.

Mount Abora: (n) a mountain range rumored to skirt mythical Xanadu.

Proteus: (n) a sea god; the son of Oceanus.

rill: (n) a small river.

scepter: (n) the authority of kingship.

scud: (v) to sail against a strong wind with no sail.

seethe: (v) to be agitated like boiling water; excited

serene: (n) tranquility

sinuous: (adj) having many curves.

smite: (v) hit.

sordid: (adj) base or vile.

suckle: (v) to nurse at the breast.

Telemachus: (n) Odysseus's son in the *Odyssey*.

thresher: (n) a person that separates the grain from the plant by beating it during harvest.

thrice: (adv) three times.

Triton: (n) the son of Poseidon.

trunkless: (adj) without a body.

twould: contraction of it would.

unburnished: (adj) metal that is not shiny.

vaulted: (v) to be thrown up high in the air.

vex: (v) to torment.

visage: (n) face.

wan: (adj) pale.

waning moon: the moon anytime after it is full.

Xanadu: Coleridge's spelling of Xandu, modern day Shangtu; the summer palace of Kublai Kahn in SE Mongolia. Because of this poem it is now associated with any mysterious place of beauty and luxury.

Study Questions

1. Reread "Kubla Khan." It uses iambic tetrameter, stressed and unstressed line of four feet. For this poem, read it out loud. Why did Coleridge use this kind of rhythm and meter?

2. Symbols are an important part of poetry where various meanings come out of the same image. "Kubla Khan" is full of imagery. What are some symbols you get from these images? Use the poem to support your answer.

3. Look at the images of the pleasure dome, the caves, and the damsel with a dulcimer. What do these images have in common symbolically?

4. Keats' poem is a Petrarchan sonnet of fourteen lines—an octet (8 lines) and a sestet (six lines). In Petrarchan sonnets the octet presents a problem, event, or situation. The sestet gives a solution to the problem or just comments on the event or situation. Explain how Keats sets up the octet and how he comments on it in the sestet. Explain your answer with specific words or images.

5. Lord Tennyson's poem is a dramatic monologue that has a character reveal a situation only through his or her point of view. Is the narrator (Ulysses) talking in the poem actually the voice of Tennyson? Or do you think Ulysses thoughts and ideas are somewhat different from Tennyson's? Explain your answer with ideas from the poem.

(See also Robert Browning's "My Last Duchess" in Theme Nine for more examples of dramatic dialogue.)

6. How does H.D. feel about Helen in the poem? Is it positive or negative? How do you know? Use examples from the poem to support your answer. Why do people hate Helen? Is this hate justified? Explain.

7. Why does Wordsworth use the mythic in his poem? What is the meaning of the mythical references in the poem?

8. According to Wordsworth, how are we to overcome the world? Should we just leave civilization and become hermits in the forest or mountains? What is it that Wordsworth is trying to say?

9. Shelley's poem is a Petrarchan poem, but it doesn't fit exactly into the mold that was established at that time. Analyze the poem again and find out what makes this poem different from other conventional Petrarchan poems.

10. Climatic moments, a time when the poet's feelings overpower him and the poem, are found throughout Shelley's poetry. Where is the climatic moment in "Ozymandias"? How does it affect the rest of the poem?

IV. THEME FOUR: VISIONS OF EVERYDAY

Introduction

Poetic Texts

Words & Phrases

Study Questions

INTRODUCTION TO THEME FOUR

Visions of Everyday

In opposition to the epic mythical view of life is the quiet everyday usage of language to basically deal with the same themes. We have seen our poets use grandiose themes and language to create concrete ideas of immaterial ideas. On the other hand, we can see that the simple language of life is just as effective as the mythic—it's just a little quieter but no less effective.

Our first glimpse into the everyday is "It Is a Beauteous Evening" by William Wordsworth. Here the narrator is walking on a beach with his daughter, enjoying the quiet sunset. "The holy time is quiet as a Nun / Breathless with adoration." In his description of the sunset, Wordsworth invokes Catholic images that make it seem they are walking in a cathedral, except this one is not manmade but devised by God. In fact, God is in the natural altar that is the sea, living and exerting his influence upon the land. "Listen! The Mighty Being is awake, / And doth with his eternal motion make / A sound like thunder—everlastingly." It is here that the narrator and daughter enjoy a stroll. While the narrator takes in the significance of man and nature, his daughter probably does not. That does not matter, however, for she, like all children, rest in "Abraham's bosom" (a very Christian metaphor for heaven) all year long. Adults must go out of their way to experience God in nature; for children, God is with them always and need not to contemplate the wonders of their surroundings.

In contrast to the safe sanctuary of nature is William Blake's (1757-1827) "The Sick Rose," which conjures nature's darker, more dangerous side. In the previous poem, we get the ideal love of a father for his child. He sees in her the quiet residence of God in contrast to the wondrous yet somewhat tempestuous nature of God. There is nothing but awe and respect for nature and humanity both. In Blake's poem, there is a sense of innocence, represented by the rose, dieing at the very hands of rascally nature. The invisible worm, somewhat symbolic of the serpent in the Garden of Eden, has secretly come by way of a howling storm to destroy the rose's virginity or innocence. As the child knows no more of God in the sea or a sunset, so the rose knows not of its destruction by the worm. There are sexual connotations in the poem that won't be explored here, but we can note the rose's "crimson joy," which is sexual in meaning and shows modern culture's attitude toward sex as seen from the Victorian age up to the present. Sex is a natural and beautiful thing that creates life and allows us to enjoy a peaceful stroll on the beach with our own children. Nevertheless, society at large has tainted and shamed the very idea and word of "sex" that it is rarely seen as love but a "dark secret love" that would make grown men and women blush. Thus, "The Sick Rose" is often seen as a symbol of rape, though it goes deeper than that.

Next is Robert Frost's (1874-1963) "The Road Not Taken." In order to understand what Frost is saying, we have to concentrate on the title. Remember, this is a poem about the road that the narrator did not walk down; it is not about "the one less traveled by." Already, in the title, there is a sense of regret. The narrator presents to us two roads that fork into the woods from the path he is taking. Both roads look about the same: one, in fact, looks a little better than the other though both paths had been traveled as much as the other. What Frost seems to be saying is that the path we choose in life is not what is really important, but why we choose it. There is a bit of sorrow over not getting to experience the "road not taken" and the narrator even mentions coming back another day to go down the second road, but "doubted if I should ever come back." He tells us this with a sigh and then says that he took the road "less traveled by, / and that has made all the difference." It is not the fact that he took the road less traveled that made the difference; it is not as simple as that because he has already told us that both roads are the same. It is probably the fact that he actually took a path and went on with his life. How many of us have faced a choice and decided not to do anything about it—we didn't take any path? We turn around and go back the way we came, uncomfortable with major decisions. I assume that "the one less traveled by" is the path forward and not backward, regardless of the choice the narrator made. It would seem that there is regret in this choice and hope that the other path with "better claim" would lead to a better future. But that is not what is important. What is important is the choice in the first place. He made his choice and is willing to live with it because he at least chose. How about us? What will we do when we are at the crossroads in our life? Will we choose? Or will we turn your back to destiny and be content with life as it is?

For A.E. Housman, when he reached a fork in the road of

his life's journey, he kept going, never looking back. In his poem "When I Was One-and-Twenty," Housman tells us that giving away worldly treasure is a lot better than giving away love. The narrator, a young twenty-one-year-old, is told by a wise man to not easily give his love away. It is easier and wiser to give treasures away than love. But what does such advice mean to a youth? Is it not better to keep money and put off love until later? This wise man would think so. What would make the wise man say this? There is a sense of unhappiness in love, perhaps out of unrequited or rejected love on account of this wise man. At the end of the first stanza, when the young man rejects the wise man's words, the second stanza is a reiteration of the first; yet more intense. "The heart out of the bosom / Was never given in vain" is a clever way of saying that when one is to fall in love, he/she should fall in love for the rest of life, and not give up one love for another. Housman, having a firm belief in loving only one person in a lifetime, felt the pains of unrequited love and never loved another person again. In fact, not until his only love died did Housman himself wilt away, his muse lost from his poetry. The narrator is telling us this at a ripe old age of twenty two.

The final poem, "Beat! Beat! Drums!" by Walt Whitman, can be classified as a war poem but has been placed in this section for the choice of everyday events in order to document the effects of war on civilians and not soldiers. Unlike the poems featured in the mythical section as well, this poem expresses the horror that the glories of war create. The rhythm and cadence of the verse along with the heart pounding start of the stanza bring to mind the magnificence and honors of war. What follows is a shopping list of death and destruction artfully written as if these kinds of activities are not much of a bother, yet the powerful words of "ruthless force" and "terrible drums" tell us otherwise. Churches and schools; newlyweds and farmers—all are affected by the cries of war that will forever change them. The everyday bustle of city streets; residents and shop owners; entertainers; lawyers and judges—all are insignificant in the tide of war. No mercy; it takes young and old, men and women alike. No matter what glories we are told of, the soldier and warrior, the beat of the drums, and the trump of the bugles sound the end of innocence and everyday affairs. It is as if all that we have read about in this section, all that we take for granted will end with the beat, beat of war drums, an important reminder, even today in an age of continued conflict outside of our borders.

William Wordsworth

It Is a Beauteous Evening

It is a beauteous evening, calm and free,
The holy time is quiet as a Nun
Breathless with adoration; the broad sun
Is sinking down in its tranquility;
The gentleness of heaven broods o'er the Sea:
Listen! the Mighty Being is awake,
And doth with his eternal motion make
A sound like thunder--everlastingly.
Dear child! dear Girl! that walkest with me here,
If thou appear untouched by solemn thought,
Thy nature is not therefore less divine:
Thou liest in Abraham's[1] bosom all the year,
And worshipp'st at the Temple's inner shrine,
God being with thee when we know it not.

---

1 The father and patriarch of the Israelites.

William Blake

The Sick Rose

O Rose, thou art sick!
The invisible worm
That flies in the night,
In the howling storm,
Has found out thy bed
Of crimson joy:
And his dark secret love
Does thy life destroy.

Robert Frost

The Road Not Taken

Two roads diverged in a yellow wood,
And sorry I could not travel both
And be one traveler, long I stood
And looked down one as far as I could
To where it bent in the undergrowth;

Then took the other, as just as fair
And having perhaps the better claim,
Because it was grassy and wanted wear;
Though as for that, the passing there
Had worn them really about the same,

And both that morning equally lay
In leaves no step had trodden black
Oh, I kept the first for another day!
Yet knowing how way leads on to way,
I doubted if I should ever come back.

I shall be telling this with a sigh
Somewhere ages and ages hence:
Two roads diverged in a wood, and I --
I took the one less traveled by,
And that has made all the difference.

A. E. Housman

When I Was One-and-Twenty

When I was one-and-twenty
  I heard a wise man say,
"Give crowns and pounds and guineas
  But not your heart away;
Give pearls away and rubies
  But keep your fancy free."
But I was one-and-twenty,
  No use to talk to me.

When I was one-and-twenty
  I heard him say again,
"The heart out of the bosom
  Was never given in vain;
'Tis paid with sighs a plenty
  And sold for endless rue.
And I am two-and-twenty,
  And oh, 'tis true, 'tis true.

Walt Whitman

Beat! Beat! Drums!

Beat! beat! drums!--Blow! bugles! blow!
Through the windows--through doors--burst like a ruthless force,
Into the solemn church, and scatter the congregation;
Into the school where the scholar is studying;
Leave not the bridegroom quiet--no happiness must he have now with his bride;
Nor the peaceful farmer any peace, plowing his field or gathering his grain;
So fierce you whirr and pound, you drums--so shrill you bugles blow.

Beat! beat! drums!--Blow! bugles! blow!
Over the traffic of cities--over the rumble of wheels in the streets:
Are beds prepared for sleepers at night in the houses? No sleepers must sleep in those beds;
No bargainers' bargains by day--no brokers or speculators—Would they continue?
Would the talkers be talking? would the singer attempt to sing?
Would the lawyer rise in the court to state his case before the judge?
Then rattle quicker, heavier drums--you bugles wilder blow.

Beat! beat! drums!--Blow! bugles! blow!
Make no parley--stop for no expostulation;
Mind not the timid--mind not the weeper or prayer;
Mind not the old man beseeching the young man;
Let not the child's voice be heard, nor the mother's entreaties;
Make even the trestles to shake the dead, where they lie awaiting the hearses,
So strong you thump, O terrible drums--so loud you bugles blow.

Words & Phrases

Abraham's bosom: (n) heaven.
beseech: (v) to beg earnestly.
bosom: (n) chest.
broker: (n) a person who buys and sells property without ever owning it; the middleman between property buyers.
brood: (v) to think or ponder heavily.
crimson: (adj) red.
crown: (n) a silver coin used in the United Kingdom before 1971.
diverge: (v) one road that breaks into two; branch off.
entreaty: (n) plea or cry in request.
expostulation: (n) a polite protest.
guinea: (n) a gold coin used in the United Kingdom before 1813.
Mighty Being: (n) God.
one-and-twenty: (n) 21 years old.
parley: (n) an informal meeting.
pound: (n) a monetary unit used in the United Kingdom.
rue: (n) sorrow or regret.
speculator: (n) a person who buys risky products at a high price in order to sell at an even higher price; a type of commodity gambler.
trestle: a beam of wood held up by four legs; used to place coffins on.
trodden: (v) past participle of tread; to walk along and crush vegetation under foot.

Study Questions

1. How do the poems in this section differ from the poems in the Mythic section? Use specific examples from poems to answer this question?

2. Which theme, mythic or everyday, do you feel creates a better mood for the theme? Explain.

3. Compare Wordsworth's "It Is a Beauteous Evening" with Blake's "Sick Rose." Both speak of passing from the world of innocence into a world of experience. Which poem relates this idea better? Explain. How do these poems compliment each other in this theme?

4. What is the symbolism behind these words: rose, worm, storm, crimson joy, and secret love? Explain. Is it really fair to say that this poem is about sexual experience and that the words listed are sexual symbols? Why or why not? What is another way to interpret the poem?

5. In "The Road Not Taken," what is the anticipation? What is the remorse?

6. The narrator in Frost's poem suddenly stops at a fork in the road. What causes the pause? Explain. What does this say about the narrator?

7. What is the advice that the wise man gives the 21-year-old narrator? What advice does he give later? Why is there

a contradiction? Is this contradiction important to understand? Explain.

8. Reread Whitman's poem. Pay close attention to the drums and bugles. In the second stanza, where do they sound? What follows after the call?

9. In the third stanza of Whitman's poem, what actions are unacceptable? What is Whitman saying must be disregarded? Why must this be so?

V. THEME FIVE: **NATURE**

Introduction
Poetic Texts
Words & Phrases
Study Questions

INTRODUCTION TO THEME FIVE

Nature

Nature, in this section, deals with life and the natural course of all things from creation or birth to destruction or death. We will see in the next section how it in some ways runs opposite to death, but, of course, all things are connected; we cannot have life without death. We will look at and discuss in depth the idea of life in nature and how humanity and culture in some way run contrary to it, either by spoiling it or destroying it. However, nature can never be viewed or enjoyed in a vacuum. There has to be interaction between us and it. What some poets have seen in nature as childlike innocence, others have expressed as raw and primitive.

In our first poem, W.B. Yeats' (1865-1939) "The Lake Isle of Innisfree," we get nature at its most idyllic. The forlorn narrator, now standing "on the pavements grey" in the bustle of our own ecosystem, the city, thinks back to the simple life at his log cabin in total isolation in the isolated ecosystem of the lake isle of Innisfree. We are lulled into a calm sense of meditation reading over the hexameter lines, lapping at the end of each line like the tranquil waves on the lake. The only noise to be heard is the buzzing of bees, the songs of the crickets, and the beating of birds' wings. The poem leads us down the path of this beautiful nature trail until we are jolted out of serenity by the contrasting words of humanity's ugly ecosystem, robbing us of peace, robbing us of warmth. Thus, the poem ends with only a memory of paradise, as all of postmodern experiences with nature becomes.

Sara Teasdale (1884-1933), in "There Will Come Soft Rains," also starts her poem with the mesmerizing role of nature. Any of us who has experienced the countryside first hand can close our eyes and experience the freshness of nature after a light rain storm. The nature that is so much a part of human experience in Yeats' poem is so much more independent in this one. By line seven, we get a sense of what is later revealed that humanity is wiped out completely. Despite all the wars, and especially nuclear annihilation that is reawakened in this decade, nature continues on, unconcerned that humanity is no longer around to enjoy its freshness and tranquility. What is especially interesting about his poem is that with all the horrid impact that war has on society, with all of humanity's achievements and ecological disaster, nature continues on without a single trace of said humanity. In fact, humanity places no importance what-so-ever in the scheme of things in the poem. All of mankind's greatest questions are actually answered in this poem. The philosopher Bishop Berkeley (1685-1753) said that minds are needed to experience nature. If a tree falls in a forest, does it make a sound? In other words, is sound a phenomenon that requires ears? Does beauty require sight? If man does not exist, can nature exist? Berkeley would essentially say no. Teasdale shows us that nature doesn't need us; we need nature.

While Teasdale's poem, no matter how beautiful, may seem a bit misanthropic, William Wordsworth brings humanity back into nature with "She Dwelt Among Untrodden Ways." Wordsworth references a female child, Lucy, as a connection children often have to nature. Later research has revealed that the "she" is in an actual child that Wordsworth knew by the name of Lucy, and he actually wrote several poems about her entitled *Lucy Poems*. In this poem, Lucy exists in a paradise that is actually free of humanity, for she lives in "untrodden ways" or a place that no one has stepped foot upon before. Wordsworth is making a connection of childhood innocence with nature. Adults often look upon a rainbow as a thing of beauty, but a child sees it as something grand and magical that there can actually be something or another world at the end of it? Children are connected to nature as much as ancient cultures were as seen by their mythology. The only tragedy is that children grow up, become adults, and either forget their connection to nature, or in some way become a part of its destruction. Though this child is dead and none may know of her, the fact that she has reminded the narrator of humanity's connection with nature is enough to praise her as being a thing of nature.

An overwhelming connection adults do have with nature is the negative aspects of it. If we go about our day without a sense of the natural beauty of the world, we are constantly aware of its grotesqueries. Thomas Hardy (1840-1928) writes of his own pessimism toward the end of the nineteenth century and his hope for the twentieth in "A Darkling Thrush." The narrator stands at a gate entering a small grove of trees and despairs over the death it has suffered at the hands of winter and frost. The place is desolate. All others are in their homes warming themselves at their fireplaces, certainly aware of nature's harshness. The narrator compares the barrenness of the scene before him with the previous century that he sees only as a corpse. The very scene of gray skies and shrunken vegetation is like a crypt, void of life. Such dreariness could not possibly produce warmth in any soul. The second half of the poem, however, becomes more upbeat with the "full-hearted evensong" of "an aged thrush, frail, gaunt, and small." There, surrounded by desolation, a lone bird sings carols creating a "happy good-night air." This not only gives hope to the narrator that the wintry nature around him could not, it also gives a reminder that with death there is rebirth, that when nature seems to have let us down, it will be there to pick us back up. In other words, we may abandon nature, but nature will never abandon us.

In sharp contrast to the thrush is Lord Alfred Tennyson's "The Eagle." Here we have a wondrous description of an eagle as both majestic and terrible. The use of alliteration (the repetition of consonants) in "He **c**lasps the **c**rag with **c**rooked hands" adds to the harshness of the description. We are faced with nothing but awe at such a creature. If we were but a miniscule animal, we would most definitely fear the majesty of this bird. Tennyson did subtitle this poem as a fragment, however, giving us something to think about—what is missing? The final line, "And like a thunderbolt he falls" can easily be written that the eagle has launched from its perch on the mountain ledge and is dropping like a thunderbolt down to some unsuspecting prey below. The "fragment" is the ambiguousness of this line. Another interpretation is that someone has shot the poor bird and it suddenly plummets to its death, reminding the reader of the majesty as well as the frailty of nature. Nature can consume us on a whim, but we can also consume it quicker and more effortlessly.

W. B. Yeats

The Lake Isle of Innisfree

I will arise and go now, and go to Innisfree,
And a small cabin build there, of clay and wattles made:
Nine bean-rows will I have there, a hive for the honey-bee,
And live alone in the bee-loud glade.

And I shall have some peace there, for peace comes dropping slow,
Dropping from the veils of the mourning to where the cricket sings;
There midnight's all a glimmer, and noon a purple glow,
And evening full of the linnet's wings.

I will arise and go now, for always night and day
I hear lake water lapping with low sounds by the shore;
While I stand on the roadway, or on the pavements grey,
I hear it in the deep heart's core.

Sara Teasdale

There Will Come Soft Rains

There will come soft rains and the smell of the ground,
And swallows circling with their shimmering sound;
And frogs in the pool singing at night,
And wild plum trees in tremulous white;
Robins will wear their feathery fire,
Whistling their whims on a low fence-wire;
And not one will know of the war, not one
Will care at last when it is done.
Not one would mind, neither bird nor tree,
If mankind perished utterly;
And Spring herself when she woke at dawn
Would scarcely know that we were gone.

William Wordsworth

She Dwelt Among Untrodden Ways

She dwelt among the untrodden ways
Beside the springs of Dove,
Maid whom there were none to praise
And very few to love:

A violet by a mossy tone
Half hidden from the eye!
Fair as a star, when only one
Is shining in the sky.

She lived unknown, and few could know
When Lucy ceased to be;
But she is in her grave, and, oh,
The difference to me!

Thomas Hardy

The Darkling Thrush

I leant upon a coppice gate
When Frost was specter-gray,
And Winter's dregs made desolate
The weakening eye of day.

The tangled bine-stems scored the sky
Like strings of broken lyres,
And all mankind that haunted nigh
Had sought their household fires.

The land's sharp features seemed to be
The Century's corpse outleant,
His crypt the cloudy canopy,
The wind his death-lament.
The ancient pulse of germ and birth
Was shrunken hard and dry,
And every spirit upon earth
Seemed fervorless as I.

At once a voice arose among
The bleak twigs overhead
In a full-hearted evensong
Of joy illimited;
An aged thrush, frail, gaunt, and small,
In blast-beruffled plume,
Had chosen thus to fling his soul

Upon the growing gloom.

So little cause for carolings
Of such ecstatic sound
Was written on terrestrial things
Afar or nigh around,
That I could think there trembled through
His happy good-night air
Some blessèd Hope, whereof he knew
And I was unaware.

Alfred, Lord Tennyson

The Eagle

He clasps the crag with crooked hands;
Close to the sun in lonely lands,
Ringed with the azure world, he stands.
The wrinkled sea beneath him crawls;
He watches from his mountain walls,
And like a thunderbolt he falls.

Words & Phrases

azure: (n) a blue sky without clouds.
bine: (n) a twining plant.
coppice: (adj) a grove of trees.
crag: (n) steep, rugged rock.
dreg: (n) small remaining amount.
evensong: (n) a prayer sung in the evening.
feathery fire: the red breast of a robin.
fervorless: (adj) without passion.
gaunt: (adj) very thin and bony.
illimited: (adj) unlimited.
lap: (v) water washing up against something.
linnet: (n) a small bird.
lyre: (n) a small stringed instrument like a harp.
nigh: (adv) close by.
plume: (n) feathers.
pulse: (n) vitality; energy; spirit.
score: (v) to cut lines into.
terrestrial: (adj) earthly.
tremulous: (adj) quivering or shaking.
wattle: (n) sticks interwoven together to make a wall.

Study Questions

1. Compare Yeats' poem "The Lake Isle of Innisfree" with the pastoral poetry encountered in our first chapter. Is there a difference between the speaker and nature in any of these poems or is there actually a connection? Explain.

2. "There Will Come Soft Rains" is also featured in Ray Bradbury's short story of the same name? Find the story on the Internet and compare the tone of the poem with the story. What is similar? What is different? How does knowledge of this poem help in the understanding of the short story? Explain.

3. Reread Wordsworth's poem. What do the metaphors of "star" and "violet" mean? How do these metaphors apply to Lucy?

4. We can read "The Darkling Thrush" literally. However, we also know that poets work in metaphor. What is a good metaphor for the darkling thrush in this poem?

5. Is it a paradox to place the darkling thrush in such a dreary landscape? Why or why not? What effect is Hardy trying to create by doing this?

6. In Theme Nine we talk about Keats' idea of negative capability? Review the meaning. Reread "The Eagle." How does Tennyson accomplish negative capability here? Use examples from the text to support your answer.

7. What is the symbolic difference between the darkling thrush and the eagle? What are they supposed to represent symbolically?

8. What do all these poems have to say about the power of nature? Can you unify them all into a single theme? Use specific examples from the poem to support your answer.?

VI. THEME SIX: DEATH

Introduction

Poetic Texts

Words & Phrases

Study Questions

INTRODUCTION TO THEME SIX

Death

Death is a subject that often brings chills to the bones and causes the heart to skip a beat. Why is it that we are so afraid of our own mortality? In a world where exploration of the unknown has occurred since the beginning of humankind, death is essentially the last frontier that not only frightens us, but allures us. This section is attached to nature as an opposing theme for the very purpose of our misconceptions of both topics. We assume nature to be full of life and positive, while death is something to fear because of the end. We have already seen that nature is just as dangerous, if not more so, than it is beautiful. As we will see in this chapter, death is but a stepping stone to something greater. The great Welsh poet Dylan Thomas (1914-1953) once wrote,

And death shall have no dominion
Dead men naked they shall be one
With the man in the wind and the west moon;
When their bones are picked clean and the clean bones gone,
They shall have stars at elbow and foot;
Though they go mad they shall be sane,
Though they sink through the sea they shall rise again;
Though lovers be lost love shall not;
And death shall have no dominion.

There could be no greater hymn to live than this one

about death. Though we all will die and our bodies decompose in the earth, eternity will be waiting for us. We may be mad or be the most pathetic, lonely person on the planet, but with death, all is restored. We may lose our parents, children, and friends, but the love we hold for each other will not be lost. Thus, with the following selection of poems, some of the greatest poets of all time have picked up a pen and tried to soothe the sad soul with alternative perspectives on the very frightening idea of death.

Our first poem, Emily Dickinson's (1830-1886) "Because I Could Not Stop For Death," shows us the narrator's trepidation with death, yet there is a beauty to it that we normally do not associate with death and funerals. The first stanza explains that the narrator did not want to die, but she has all the same; she uses a carriage as a metaphor for death that carries her away. The journey is slow and she can only observe. She feels like she is moving, but it is life that is actually moving on; this is the first time in her "life" she has ever had time, for death makes time for all. The fourth stanza describes the death shroud she is dressed in (her gossamer gown), and the fifth stanza describes the house that is "a swelling of the ground," the tomb where she will live for eternity. Here, in death, time has no meaning, and centuries feel like minutes. Though the narrator is dead, there is no fear in her words, only peace.

John Donne's "Holy Sonnet 10" deals with the paradox of death for the religious. Why is it that a person who believes in a glorious afterlife should be so afraid of it? Does this fear show lack of belief? Though Donne could not answer these questions definitively, he did try to address them in his poetry. In literature, Death is often a figure to be feared, and, as in John Milton's *Paradise Lost*, Death is even greater than Satan while having the power to even harm him. Donne only scoffs at that image. His poem explains the absolute powerlessness Death actually has over us. We all die, but it is a gate to a greater place. This horrible apparition that is Death is merely a slave of "fate, chance, kings, and desperate men" who are the ones that actually decide who will live or die, and not Death himself. Death's only companions, it turns out, are "poison, war, and sickness," but we can imitate death with certain drugs (the poppy) and charms (hypnotism), so what is so special about what death does? While we go on to live for eternity through Christ's resurrection, Death will eventually end, and he, not us, shall die.

George Herbert's (1593-1633) "Death" takes the idea of Christ's resurrection and its effect on Death a little further. Remember that both Donne and Herbert were priests who used poetry as a way to preach. Their poems are often sermons to the faithful, so the Christian imagery is often overbearing. Broken into six stanzas, the first three stanzas of "Death" deal with the overall historical perception of death as skeletal, for that is what becomes of us all "some six / Or ten years hence" from death. The overall tone of these stanzas is one of dread and disgust, where even Death is somber, and, unlike Donne's initial view, is far from proud. The final three stanzas deal with how Christ's sacrifice has beautified death. No longer should death be perceived as rotting and wasted, but lovely and angelical. Death, as Herbert pictures him now, is a happy soul, rejoicing in the death of all, not because it is the end but the beginning of something new and better. The final stanza gives a hidden warning, though. When we die, we still trust that we will go to a better place, but can we? It all depends upon how we live our life here and now.

Despite the positive spin Donne and Herbert try to put on death as being a doorway to eternal happiness, there is no arguing the fact that death is tragic in our world and time, and the loss of a loved one has a deep impact on our lives, especially psychologically. Walt Whitman's "O Captain! My Captain!" is a fitting eulogy written after the assassination of Abraham Lincoln. Utilizing apostrophe, a figure of speech where the narrator directly speaks to someone not present, Whitman gives adoration to Lincoln, whose loss shocked the nation. Whitman spoke about how he had a dream of a ship under full sail entering the harbor the night before Lincoln was shot. Whitman couples the ship entering port imagery with President Lincoln as the captain of the ship, which represents the newly won Union of the American states. Lincoln, as the captain, has survived the tumultuous storm (The Civil War) that almost destroyed his vessel (America). Just as he nears the port (the end of the war), he is received as a hero; but, to the dismay of those waiting, he has "fallen cold and dead" on the deck of his ship. The second stanza is the narrator's wish that the death of such a great man, who turns out to be his father, is only a dream as he hold's the captain in his arms. The third stanza reaffirms it is not a dream, but the death of the captain was not in vain. Though the ship has come to port with the leader now passed on, the ultimate goal of the ship returning safely has been accomplished. Whitman's tone and use of words such as "fallen cold and dead" deepen the tragedy of death for such a revered person, but there is also hope in the poem as well, for no matter how we die, it is how we live our life that is of utmost importance.

If Whitman's poem is a good example of how we mourn the passing of loved or revered ones, William Shakespeare's (1564-1616) Sonnet 71, shows us how we should move on. The narrator's view of life is a negative one where he sees this world as "vile" and fallen where "vile worms" feed on our bodies after we die. Because he loves the person to whom this poem is written, he would rather have them forget him than to mourn over him and live in misery. He would rather have the love for him decay as his body decays. Otherwise, people will use the misery over his death against the lover and mock him/her. If this is the case, who will stand to defend? The theme in this poem captures a nihilistic view of love and death, one that is the exact opposite of Whitman's. For the narrator of this poem, love is just as much a burden as death, for both cause a person to suffer, and when we suffer, we are the most exposed to the ruthless abuse of others.

Emily Dickinson

Because I Could Not Stop For Death

Because I could not stop for Death—
He kindly stopped for me—
The Carriage held but just Ourselves—
And Immortality.

We slowly drove—He knew no haste
And I had put away
My labor and my leisure too,
For His Civility—

We passed the School, where Children strove
At Recess—in the Ring—
We passed the Fields of Gazing Grain—
We passed the Setting Sun—

Or rather—He passed Us—
The Dews drew quivering and chill—
For only Gossamer, my Gown—
My Tippet—only Tulle—

We paused before a House that seemed
A Swelling of the Ground—
The Roof was scarcely visible—
The Cornice—in the Ground—

Since then—'tis Centuries—and yet

Feels shorter than the Day
I first surmised the Horses' Heads
Were toward Eternity—

John Donne

Death Be Not Proud

Death, be not proud, though some have callèd thee
Mighty and dreadful, for thou art not so;
For those whom thou thinkst, thou dost overthrow
Die not, poor death, nor yet canst thou kill me.
From rest and sleep, which but thy pictures be,
Much pleasure—then from thee much more must flow,
And soonest our best men with thee do go,
Rest of their bones, and soul's delivery.
Thou art slave to fate, chance, kings, and desperate men,
And dost with poison, war, and sickness dwell,
And poppy or charms can make us sleep as well,
And better then thy stroke; why swellst thou then?
One short sleep past, we wake eternally
And death shall be no more; Death, thou shalt die.

George Herbert

Death

Death, thou wast once an uncouth hideous thing,
Nothing but bones,
The sad effect of sadder groans:
Thy mouth was open, but thou couldst not sing.

For we considered thee as at some six
Or ten years hence,
After the loss of life and sense,
Flesh being turned to dust, and bones to sticks.

We looked on this side of thee, shooting short,
Where we did find
The shells of fledge-souls left behind—
Dry dust, which sheds no tears, but may extort.

But since our Savior's death did put some blood
Into thy face,
Thou art grown fair and full of grace,
Much in request, must sought for as a good.

For we do now behold thee gay and glad,
As at doomsday,
When souls shall wear their new array,
And all thy bones with beauty shall be clad.

Therefore we can go die as sleep, and trust

Half that we have
Unto an honest faithful grave,
Making our pillows either down or dust.

Walt Whitman

O CAPTAIN! MY CAPTAIN!

O Captain! my Captain, our fearful trip is done,
The ship has weather'd every rack, the prize we sought is won,
The port is near, the bells I hear, the people all exulting,
While follow eyes the steady keel, the vessel grim and daring;
But O heart! heart! heart!
O the bleeding drips of red,
Where on the deck my Captain lies,
Fallen cold and dead.

O Captain! my Captain! rise up and hear the bells;
Rise up—for you the flag is flung—for you the bugle trills,
For you bouquets and ribbon'd wreaths—for you the shores a-crowding,
For you they call, the swaying mass, their eager faces turning;
Here Captain! dear father!
This arm beneath your head!
It is some dream that on the deck,
You've fallen cold and dead.

My Captain does not answer, his lips are pale and still,
My father does not feel my arm, he has no pulse nor will,
The ship is anchor'd safe and sound, its voyage closed and done,

From fearful trip the victor ship comes in with object won;
Exult O shores, and ring O bells!
But I with mournful tread,
Walk the deck my Captain lies,
Fallen Cold and Dead.

William Shakespeare

No Longer Mourn For Me

No longer mourn for me when I am dead
Than you shall hear the surly sullen bell
Give warning to the world that I am fled
From this vile world, with vilest worms to dwell:
Nay, if you read this line, remember not
The hand that writ it; for I love you so,
That I in your sweet thoughts would be forgot,
If thinking on me then should make you woe.
O, if (I say) you look upon this verse,
When I perhaps compounded am with clay,
Do not so much as my poor name rehearse;
But let your love even with my life decay:
　　Lest the wise world should look into your moan,
　　And mock you with me after I am gone.

Words & Phrases

art: (v) old form of are; 2nd person singular of Be.

clad: (v) past participle of clothed.

compound: (v) to put in; combine

cornice: (n) a ledge that crowns the top of a building.

dwell: (v) live.

extort: (v) to force someone to do something i.e. death causes people to cry.

exulting: (v) to rejoice.

fledge-soul: (n) a soul that has moved on.

keel: (n) often referred to as a ship in literature.

poppy: (n) a plant with red flowers that produces a narcotic.

rack: (n) violent twist.

shell: (n) the body.

strove: (v) past tense of strive; to make an effort.

surly: (adj) unfriendly.

tippet: (n) a fur or wool scarf.

trill: (v) to call out.

tulle: (n) a net veil, perhaps worn at funerals.

uncouth: (adj) without manners.

weather: (v) to withstand the effects of terrible weather.

Study Questions

1. You may notice that Emily Dickinson's poems are composed rather differently than other poems. What is the difference exactly? How does this difference add or distract from her poem? Use examples from the poem.

2. How does Dickinson approach death? What is her opinion? Use examples from the poem? Is there a connection between death and nature or are they separate? Explain.

3. A couplet contains two lines in a poem that usually rhyme. Sonnets contain a final couplet that emphasizes the poet's point. Elizabethan sonnets became the fashion of the day with very stark couplets that stood out from the rest of the poem. The masters of the Elizabethan sonnets were, foremost, Shakespeare and Donne. Reread both their sonnets. Who do you think has the best sonnet? Why? Is there a difference in style?

4. John Donne wrote some great sonnets. Reread "Death Be Not Proud," and focus upon the couplets in line 3, 4 and 13, 14. Do you find these couplets shocking? Why or why not? What is Donne trying to say with this sonnet? Does it show his own personal religious view? Why does Donne boast that death cannot kill him? And how can death die? Does this poem give you hope or despair? Explain why?

5. Compare Herbert's poem to Donne's. What is similar

between the poems? What is different? Explain both your answers.

6. Whitman's poem is said to also form an image as a concrete poem (see chapter 10). What image do you see in his poem? How does this image fit with the overall meaning of the poem?

7. Why would the narrator in Shakespeare's poem not want anyone to mourn for him after he is gone?

8. Reread Shakespeare's poem. Why would people mock a person for expressing sorrow for another?

9. State some specific examples from the poems of how nature and death contrast each other. Also state some specific examples of how nature and death actually parallel each other.

PART II

PARALLELS

VII. THEME SEVEN:
PERSONAL INDENTITY

Introduction

Poetic Texts

Words & Phrases

Study Questions

INTRODUCTION TO THEME SEVEN

Personal Identity

Leaving opposing themes behind, we now pick up with parallel themes. These themes each have their own distinct ideas and voice but have comparable themes. The first theme we will deal with is "Personal Identity." The following poems all explore the circumstances under which a person at one time in life is still the same person at another time even though the outer appearances change.

Human life has basically been separated into three stages: youth, middle age, and old age. To the youth, the elderly appear to be from a different time, a different age, even alien, but do the youth ever sit back and think what they will be like when they are older? John Milton in "How Soon Hath Time" reminds us how fast time catches up and is the "subtle thief of youth." The narrator is in his sixties and feels that he has nothing to show at the start of his golden years. He bemoans the fact that his outward appearance cannot possibly show his feelings inside that he feels he has just reached manhood. Though he may be judged to be beyond worth, God can only judge that, so he will accomplish what is ever needed and whatever fate has in store for him. This type of poem echoes what the philosopher John Locke (1632-1704) would later clarify as consciousness that is the foundation of personal identity and not the body. Since we all will reach the phase of old age sooner or later, we need to judge a person's worth by what this very identity is and not by age or outer semblance.

Another form of personal identity is art as an extension of the creative self. Those who create for art's sake and not for money or fame view their creations as a part of themselves that do not belong to anybody else. In fact, nobody can really understand the creation better than the creator. W.B. Yeats' "A Coat" explores this idea of art as a song he has created. He uses the metaphor that his creation fits him as a coat and the embroidery that makes it beautiful has been crafted out of things from his past that he can readily identify with. However, when others come along and take his coat, which he has put a lot of time and effort into so that it looks appealing; they wear it and show it off as if they were special. This is similar to academics who sit around all day quoting their favorite poets, sounding important and learned, but have done nothing creative themselves. It is even similar to when we sing famous songs of our favorite pop artists, showing our prowess with a song that is, in fact, not our own. We have created nothing, and yet many envy our skill at wearing another's beautiful coat. Yeats says, however, to let these people have the coat. It actually shows their own uncreativeness, while he would rather go naked, for there is more complication and risk in the very act of not creating. Such an act would eventually equal out where all then would have to go naked, having no skill to make their own coat, yet the artist still remains an artist, while everyone else is just naked!

The resentment in Yeats' poem is handled rather lightly and jokingly. There is no form of malice toward the unartistic who parade around with his ideas. In fact, the narrator seems almost forgiving. William Blake, however, gives us a completely different view of how a person reacts to another who has encroached upon his own personal space. The narrator is angry with both a friend and an enemy. When he expresses his anger to his friend, the rift is healed, and his anger ends. But he hides his anger from his enemy, an anger that grows into a tree that yields a poisonous fruit upon which his enemy will eat and die from. This simple poem expresses the complex hypocritical duality we all hold within our psyche. What is often a tragedy of human life is the fact that anger is suppressed by hate. Anger is a healthy way of dealing with those who have wronged us. Hate is unhealthy for, like the poem, it is secret and destructive not only to those who are hated but to the hater as well. While the hater shrivels up inside and becomes bitter and loathing, the object of that hate continues on oblivious to the hate. When the two meet, the hater smiles and talks nicely, and then curses that same person behind his or her back. Thus, by the end of the poem, when the object of that hate lies dead, the hater feels victorious. But victory is never achieved out of hate. There are no winners, and, as this poem stresses, both suffer enormously in the end.

Perhaps Stephen Crane expresses the suffering of the hater best in his poem "The Heart." In fact, this poem could be subtitled "The Poison Tree—The Day After" so close are the two in themes. If "The Poison Tree" deals with one's anger toward another, then "The Heart" deals with one's anger toward oneself. It is written as simply and clearly as Blake's poem, and yet the depth that it reaches is great. When one has become bitter with another, what is left of his or her heart? Bitterness. Not only that, but that person has become "naked," as in revealed to all the world. In the end, when the hater has unleashed revenge upon that which is hated, who is the true monster? The hater, who has become "bestial," is feeding upon his or her own heart as if there were nothing else to feed upon. After the object of one's hate has moved on, what is left to hate? Thus this poem is about self-loathing, where the bitter heart is delicious because it is one's own.

These last two poems are a reality although a bit dark in our understanding of personal identity. On the other hand, does bitterness only lead us down to self loathing or is there a way out? Claude McKay's "America" shows us another way. Claude McKay (1889-1948) was an immigrant from Jamaica and came to the fore during the Harlem Renaissance in the 1920's. This poem captures all the bitterness of living in America but refuses to be bitter. The narrator shows what it was like to be black and poor in America: starvation, violence, and stealing for food, yet he loves the experience it gave him to make him a better person. He personifies America as a tiger, and the imagery of it as it "sinks into my throat her tiger's tooth" is both powerful and graphic. Such violence against him can only make him stronger. He doesn't debase himself to fall victim to his hate as the previous two narrators have done, but allows it to empower him against the hardships that he faces in order to survive and succeed. The love/hate relationship the narrator has with his home has the power to destroy him or make him stronger, and since personal identity is what is inside more than what is out, his own consciousness of how he reacts to his surroundings is paramount to a better life.

John Milton

How Soon Hath Time

How soon hath Time, the subtle thief of youth,
Stol'n on his wing my three and twentieth year!
My hasting days fly on with full career,
But my late spring no bud or blossom shew'th.
Perhaps my semblance might deceive the truth,
That I to manhood am arrived so near,
And inward ripeness doth much less appear,
That some more timely-happy spirits endu'th.
Yet be it less or more, or soon or slow,
It shall be still in strictest measure even
To that same lot, however mean or high,
Toward which Time leads me, and the will of Heaven;
All is, if I have grace to use it so,
As ever in my great Taskmaster's eye.

W.B. Yeats

A Coat

I made my song a coat
Covered with embroideries
Out of old mythologies
From heel to throat;
But the fools caught it,
Wore it in the world's eyes
As though they'd wrought it.
Song, let them take it,
For there's more enterprise
In walking naked.

William Blake

A Poison Tree

I was angry with my friend:
I told my wrath, my wrath did end.
I was angry with my foe;
I told it not, my wrath did grow.

And I watered it in fears,
Night & morning with my tears;
And I sunnèd it with my smiles
And with soft deceitful wiles.

And it grew both day and night,
Till it bore an apple bright;
And my foe beheld it shine,
And he knew that it was mine,

And into my garden stole
When the night had veiled the pole:
In the morning glad I see
My foe outstretched beneath the tree

Stephen Crane

The Heart

In the desert
I saw a creature, naked, bestial,
Who, squatting upon the ground,
Held his heart in his hands,
And ate of it.

I said, "Is it good, friend?"
“It is bitter-- bitter,” he answered;
“But I like it
Because it is bitter,
And because it is my heart.”

Claude McKay

America

Although she feeds me bread of bitterness,
And sinks into my throat her tiger's tooth,
Stealing my breath of life, I will confess
I love this cultured hell that tests my youth!
Her vigor flows like tides into my blood,
Giving me strength erect against her hate.
Her bigness sweeps my being like a flood,
Yet as a rebel fronts a king in state,
I stand within her walls with not a shred
Of terror, malice, not a word of jeer.
Darkly I gaze into the days ahead,
And see her might and granite wonders there,
Beneath the touch of Time's unerring hand,
Like priceless treasures sinking in the sand.

Words & Phrases

cultured hell: probably American suburbia.
embroidery: (n) designs sewn into clothing.
endu'th: (v) endure.
semblance: (n) the outward appearance.
stole: (v) past tense, to move quietly into a place.
subtle: (adj) cunning or crafty.
Taskmaster: (n) God.
three and twentieth year: (n) twenty third year.
unerring: (adj) not to be in error.
wile: (n) trickery.
wrought: (v) old form of worked; made.

Study Questions

1. What is the main point of Milton's poem? What is he lamenting? Use examples from the poem to support your answer.

2. In Yeats' "The Coat," he writes, "I made my song a coat / Covered with embroideries / Out of old mythologies / From heel to throat." Explain what this sentence means? What are the mythologies that make the embroidery of his "coat"? What do you think his coat is a metaphor for?

3. Look at the title of Blake's "A Poison Tree." What effect does the poet create by putting two contradictory ideas together?

4. Read Blake's poem carefully. Notice the pronoun "it." How many times is "it" used? What does "it" mean? How does "it" metamorphose through the poem? (i.e. what does "it" start out as and what does "it" end as?)

5. Why do you think the narrator never tells us the exact reason for his wrath in Blake's poem? Does that tell us something about the narrator?

6. Give an example of when you let your "wrath" grow until it became "poison." Of course it doesn't have to lead to disastrous consequences, but we all bottle our anger until it explodes on someone.

7. Who or what do you think the creature is in Crane's poem "The Heart"? Why would the creature find his own bitter heart delicious?

8. Reread Crane's poem. When the narrator sees the creature eating the heart, he says, "I said, 'Is it good, friend?'" Why would the narrator ask such a question? Doesn't it seem odd? What can we learn about the narrator from this one line in context to the rest of the poem?

9. Compare Crane's "The Heart" with Blake's "The Poison Tree." Are they similar in theme? Why or why not? Could the narrator's in both poems be the same person? Why or why not?

10. How can the narrator of McKay's "America" love the country that hurts him and tears him apart?

11. What does this poem say about racism? How does the narrator overcome racism? Use specific examples in your answer.

12. Since Claude McKay's poem is a sonnet, what is revealed in the last couplet?

VIII. THEME EIGHT: SOLITUDE

INTRODUCTION TO THEME EIGHT

Solitude

Solitude as a word carries negative connotations. We often think that being alone is a form of punishment. That may be true for long term isolation, but we often value short term seclusion when we need a break from work or other people. We often seek physical solitude to remove any form of interference in order to think more clearly or even meditate. Mental solitude is the state we reach when we no longer need to isolate ourselves from the world but can turn inward with high levels of concentration. Regardless of how we find inner quiet, solitude is an important part of the arts, and this section showcases various poets' opinion on the very idea of solitude itself.

Alexander Pope's (1688-1744) "Ode on Solitude" illustrates the importance of finding solitude outside the "rage of courts, and noise of towns" of city life and the easiness and purity of rural life. As an ode, Pope wanted to write a type of majestic lyrical verse directed to the very idea of solitude and what it means. This type of theme fits into the bucolic, a type of pastoral poem that eulogizes life in the country as being preferable to that in the city. The narrator sings praises to the country life and to the joys of being isolated from the city. The noise of urban life is contrasted with the sounds of the rural and the very idea that time can slip by without so much as stress or disharmony. The solitary life of country living is so quintessential, so meditative that he would rather live and die in obscurity in the country than in notoriety in the city.

This type of poem contrasts rather well the blessing of a pure life in the country compared to a more damaging and biting lifestyle in society.

Similar to an ode, which was originally a song form in classical Greek, is a hymn that conveys emotions religiously. In James Thomson's (1700-1748) "Hymn on Solitude," the narrator praises the ideal of solitude as a religious undertaking. Solitude becomes an idea practiced by "the wise and good" and avoided by "the heard of fools, and villains." In fact, the narrator often retires to solitude in order to meditate and to listen to the "truths" such solitaire brings, which has the power to break those who have created resistances to moral influences. The second stanza poetically lists different instances of solitary bliss to be sought including sleep, where mysteries are revealed; sheep herding, where songs are created on a musical pipe; love, where passion is exchanged; friendship, where beauty is enjoyed. The third stanza continues with the list with solitude being found in the morning, where plants are blessed with dew and bloom; in a forest during the heat of noon; and most poignant is the evening when the landscape dims in the twilight where the muse of creativity is at its height. The fourth stanza shifts into musing on the evening sky and religion being born from such solitary speculation. The fifth stanza is bucolic in form, for it is in London that the narrator tries the same meditation and realizes that the only place to find real solitude is back in the wilderness.

The previous poets have mostly concentrated on the positive side of solitude in a rural setting. T.S. Eliot's (1888-1965) poem "The Winter Evening Settles Down" focuses in on the negative aspect of feeling solitude within the grimy winter streets of an English city. When we think of winter, it is usually a refreshing image of peace and tranquility surrounded by a blanket of crystal white snow. There is no such feeling is Eliot's poem. Winter in England is far from enjoyable; it is often cold and bitter. Add a winter rain and it turns down right miserable. To top it off, add the grime and garbage of a city street and the solitary narrator is at a loss for inspiration. This was written near the end of World War I, when cities like London were locked in war and overwhelmed by industrialization. Eliot wonderfully describes the burnt-out cigarettes, grimy garbage, withered leaves, and broken blinds and chimney pots to conjure a world of sterility and destruction. Unlike the previous poems, there is no escape from this dreary world of mundane living. Nature does not exist except for the giddy cab horse, only solitude and misery reigns. Even the lighting of the lamps at the very end of the poem offers no hope, only an impression of septic light saturating the soot stained snow on a cold and bitter evening of dread.

Thomas Hardy creates a very atmospheric feeling of what solitude really is in his poem about the supposedly unsinkable *Titanic*. In the first five stanzas of "The Convergence of the Twain," Hardy deals with the solitude of the vessel under the waves, and in the last six stanzas, he deals with its solitude while afloat. In the cold depths of the sea surrounded by boundless primal nature, the *Titanic* wallows in a grave of luxuriant waste. The life giving warmth of its internal fires is now extinguished and cold. Life does not exist here. The opulent mirrors that once reflected beauty now reveal the “grotesque, slimed, dumb, indifferent” sea worms. Even the jewels, of which the only purpose is to draw the eyes attention to the bearer, have no purpose but to display the waste of human lust. Within the *Titanic* before the tragedy, solitude and meditation was something utterly avoided and teemed with people that the life rafts were not sufficient. Where are these people now? Where is the life and joy associated with the vessel? This symbol of Britain’s industrialization, power, and wealth is what Hardy focuses on as being hollow. Here in the solitude of the seas, what is humankind? According to this poem, nothing, for long after humanity is gone, their only legacy will be that which they leave behind. Technology and scientific advancement mean nothing compared to the power and majesty of nature. Isn’t it time we took some time to contemplate our own role as well and discover what really matters?

Alexander Pope

Ode on Solitude

I.

How happy he, who free from care
  The rage of courts, and noise of towns;
Contented breaths his native air,
          In his own grounds.

II.

Whose herds with milk, whose fields with bread,
  Whose flocks supply him with attire,
Whose trees in summer yield him shade,
          In winter fire.

III.

Blest! who can unconcern'dly find
  Hours, days, and years slide swift away,
In health of body, peace of mind,
          Quiet by day,

IV.

Sound sleep by night; study and ease
  Together mixed; sweet recreation,
And innocence, which most does please,
          With meditation.

V.

Thus let me live, unheard, unknown;
  Thus unlamented let me die;

Steal from the world, and not a stone
Tell where I lie.

James Thomson

Hymn on Solitude

Hail, mildly pleasing solitude,
Companion of the wise and good;
But, from whose holy, piercing eye,
The herd of fools, and villains fly.
Oh! how I love with thee to walk,
And listen to thy whispered talk,
Which innocence, and truth imparts,
And melts the most obdurate hearts.

A thousand shapes you wear with ease,
And still in every shape you please.
Now wrapped in some mysterious dream,
A lone philosopher you seem;
Now quick from hill to vale you fly,
And now you sweep the vaulted sky;
A shepherd next, you haunt the plain,
And warble forth your oaten strain;
A lover now, with all the grace
Of that sweet passion in your face:
Then, calmed to friendship, you assume
The gentle-looking Hertford's bloom,
As, with her Musidora, she,
(Her Musidora fond of thee)
Amid the long withdrawing vale,
Awakes the rivaled nightingale.

Thine is the balmy breath of morn,
Just as the dew-bent rose is born;
And while meridian fervors beat,
Thine is the woodland dumb retreat;
But chief, when evening scenes decay,
And the faint landskip swims away,
Thine is the doubtful soft decline,
And that best hour of musing thine.

Descending angels bless thy train,
The virtues of the sage, and swain;
Plain Innocence in white arrayed,
Before thee lifts her fearless head:
Religion's beams around thee shine,
And cheer thy glooms with light divine:
About thee sports sweet Liberty;
And rapt Urania sings to thee.

Oh, let me pierce thy secret cell!
And in thy deep recesses dwell!
Perhaps from Norwood's oak-clad hill,
When meditation has her fill,
I just may cast my careless eyes
Where London's spiry turrets rise,
Think of its crimes, its cares, its pain,
Then shield me in the woods again.

T.S. Eliot

The Winter Evening Settles Down

The winter evening settles down
With smells of steaks in passageways.
Six o'clock.
The burnt-out ends of smoky days.
And now a gusty shower wraps
The grimy scraps
Of withered leaves across your feet
And newpapers from vacant lots;
The showers beat
On empty blinds and chimney-pots,
And at the corner of the street
A lonely cab-horse steams and stamps.

And then the lighting of the lamps.

Thomas Hardy

The Convergence of the Twain

Lines on the Loss of the "Titanic"

I

In a solitude of the sea
Deep from human vanity,
And the Pride of Life that planned her, stilly couches she.

II

Steel chambers, late the pyres
Of her salamandrine fires,
Cold currents thrid, and turn to rhythmic tidal lyres.

III

Over the mirrors meant
To glass the opulent
The sea-worm crawls-grotesque, slimed, dumb, indifferent.

IV

Jewels in joy designed
To ravish the sensuous mind
Lie lightless, all their sparkles bleared and black and blind.

V

Dim moon-eyed fishes near
Gaze at the gilded gear

And query: "What does this vaingloriousness down here?"...

VI

Well: while was fashioning
This creature of cleaving wing,
The Immanent Will that stirs and urges everything

VII

Prepared a sinister mate
For her - so gaily great -
A Shape of Ice, for the time far and dissociate.

VIII

And as the smart ship grew
In stature, grace, and hue,
In shadowy silent distance grew the Iceberg too.

IX

Alien they seemed to be:
No mortal eye could see
The intimate welding of their later history,

X

Or sign that they were bent
By paths coincident
On being anon twin halves of one august event,

XI

Till the Spinner of the Years

Said "Now!" And each one hears,
And consummation comes, and jars two hemispheres.

Words & Phrases

anon: (adv) old form of at once.
attire: (n) clothes.
august: (adj) inspiring reverence.
balmy: (adj) refreshing.
bleared: (adj) to be not clear.
cell: (n) a small room.
Convergence of the Twain: bringing the two together into one.
dissociate: (v) separate.
dumb: (adj) silent.
fervor: (n) great heat.
gilded: (adj) to be coated with gold.
Hertford: (n) a city in SE England.
Immanent Will: (n) God.
impart: (v) to make known.
landskip: (n) old form for landscape.
meridian: (n) noon; 12 pm.
morn: (n) morning.
Musidora: (n) a woman often found in James Thomson's poetry.
oaten strain: possibly a pastoral song.
obdurate: (adj) pitiless.
opulent: (adj) rich.
pyre: (n) a pile of wood for burning.
rapt: (adj) to be filled with emotion.
rivaled: (adj) competing.
salamandrine: (adj) from salamander, a mythical lizard that could live in fire.

Shape of Ice: (n) the iceberg that sunk the Titanic.

Spinner of the Years: (n) possibly God.

spiry: (adj) to have a lot of spires.

stilly: (adv) silently.

swain: (n) a country boy.

third: (v) thread.

train: (n) the part of dress that trails behind the wearer.

turret: (n) a small tower on a building.

Urania: (n) the muse of astronomy.

vaingloriousness: (adj) to have excessive pride over one's own achievements.

vaulted: (adj) providing a ceiling.

warble: (v) yodel; sing with frequent changes of voice

Study Questions

1. An ode is usually a lengthy lyrical poem using lofty language through formalized stanzas. Odes were originally taken from the Greek, which means “song,” but the Greek form of the ode was seldom used in English. Instead, two other forms were adapted, the homostrophic ode and the irregular ode. Homostrophic odes, as the name implies (HOMO=SAME; STROPH=STANZA), contains stanzas of the same length and identical rhythm; while the irregular ode follows the poet’s artistic and emotional needs, following neither set rhythm nor length, i.e. Coleridge’s “Dejection: An Ode” and Wordsworth’s “Ode: Intimations of Immortality.”

Reread Pope’s “Solitude: An Ode.” Which English ode form does it follow? What is the rhyme scheme of this ode? Are the stanzas the same length? Does an ode have to be long and elevated to be effective? Why or why not? (See also Shelley’s “Ode to the West Wind” in Theme Eleven for an example of a homostrophic ode).

2. Pope was an Augustan Poet, those who return to forms of the classics, especially the Roman poets who lived under the rule of Augustus. His poetry is neo-classical in that he attempts to imitate the classical poets of Virgil, Horace, and Ovid. Therefore, the poems Pope wrote tried to follow the strict rules of rhyme and meter where the common language was replaced with a very intellectual voice, for the classical poets used poetry to express reason rather than emotion.

Reread Pope's ode. What era does he seem to praise? Does the subject matter seem real? Does the language feel like everyday speech? Explain. How do you feel when you read this poem?

3. Reread James Thomson's "A Hymn on Solitude." Is it thematically similar to Pope's? Explain with specific examples. How is it different than Pope's?

4. How do you feel when you read T.S. Eliot's poem? What specific words or phrases create these feelings?

5. What is Thomas Hardy trying to say about the culture of his time? How does that culture create loneliness and solitude?

6. What does the *Titanic* represent in Hardy's poem? What is the metaphor of the *Titanic*?

7. Express your own views on solitude. Use examples from the poems to support your answer.

8. How is the previous chapter on personal identity a parallel of solitude? Use examples from the poems to support your answer.

IX. THEME NINE: ART

Introduction

Poetic Texts

Words & Phrases

Study Questions

INTRODUCTION TO THEME NINE

Art

Poetry is an art form, what we would call the Arts or the Humanities, but we are also going to look at how poetry portrays great works of art in words separate from form. What usually makes a work of art great is the value it has aesthetically and the influence it creates emotionally. The reason most people have difficulty understanding why a painting, sculpture, or a piece of literature is so wonderful is that they do not understand the symbols and ideas behind it. Art is more than a representation of the world around us; it is the fundamental understanding of it. As in all aspects of life, we are not simply to understand art, we are to know it.

We start our study of art with Robert Browning's (1812-1889) "My Last Duchess." The poem both starts and ends on works of art, the first being a fresco of the Duke of Ferrerra's, the narrator's, now dead wife. Frescos are works of watercolor painted directly on a plaster wall, which juxtaposes the idea that art and the object of art are both seen as something to posses. The poem reveals the Duke's controlling nature over his wife, and if he cannot possess her in life, he can just as easily possess her in death through art. Possession of art symbolizes some control over the subject matter. Read carefully how he describes the beauty of the painting and compare it with how he feels for his now dead wife. The painting is a rather romanticized idea of what his wife should have been—a beautiful, silent creature for him to admire. More interesting is the Duke's own opinion of himself and the portrait he "paints" of himself as he talks to the listener. This poem reads like we are watching a play because it is written as a dramatic monologue, which has a narrator speaking to another character at a critical instant in time that reveals his or her private thoughts to the listener. Though he is talking about works of art, it is the information he reveals that becomes the focus of the poem. Though art is what they are looking at, life is what is revealed. Thus, a beautiful young woman that is of a lower class but came with a great dowry, is found difficult to control. When she is discovered flirting with other men, the Duke gives "commands" and has her killed. Yet he feels no remorse because there is another woman with a large dowry to pursue, and he can proudly gaze upon his "last Duchess painted on the wall" and boast of her whenever he feels. It just so happens that the person he is talking to is an emissary for another Duke looking to give his daughter away for marriage. Finally, at the end of the poem, we see the second work of art, a bronze statue of Neptune taming a sea-horse. Again, the Duke's psyche is revealed through a work of art, mainly that he sees himself as Neptune and women as the sea-horse.

Where Browning's poem dealt with art as an outward object, Archibald Macleish (1892-1982) deals with art as an inward expression. "Ars Poetica" is Latin for the art of poetry, and it is interesting that Macleish deals with the art of poetry through the form of a poem. Since it is near impossible to paint or sketch the "art" of poetry, the only appropriate way to draw a picture of a poem in our mind is through words. Unlike many poets or painters, Macleish avoids romanticizing his object. By calling a poem "mute", "dumb", and "wordless," Macleish tries to illustrate the irregularities of this art form. The paradoxes easily show us poetry can be motionless and still progress "as the moon climbs;" it can be "silent as the sleeve-worn stone" yet still have something to say; it can be sterile in look and form yet be as delicious and fulfilling "as a globed fruit." Therefore, by the time we reach the end of the poem, we are reminded that "A poem should not mean / But be." We should realize that poetry and art are not just created to be analyzed but for artistic edification. Now stop thinking about the poems and just let them flow!

Marianne Moore (1887-1972) seems to take what Macleish said in "Ars Poetica" and proves it. In "Poetry," Moore both speaks her contempt for the rigid form that poetry seems to impose upon the artist and yet still praise poetry for its grandeur and sophistication. "Poetry" may appear to be written in free verse, a style of poetry lacking strict meter and rhyme and with total disregard to form or meter, but a closer inspection of her poem reveals strict adherence to form with some rhyme and rhythm. In fact, Moore makes a rather good point that free verse isn't as "free" as the term implies. Her poem is still verse, and it still looks and reads as a poem as compared to a short story. Moore has succeeded in writing a poem about poetry in such a way that it resembles what Tristan Tzara attempted to do with Dadaism, a movement started after World War I in an attempt to break art from idea and statement; or more famously what Picasso did with Cubism. Can we call "Poetry" poetry if it so flagrantly breaks all the norms and rules established before? Is Moore indignant of what poetry has become? The answer lies in the form through which she protests and praises the art of poetry itself. Just as Picasso breathed new life into art through his informal style, so has Moore managed to courageously express her own contempt and admiration of an art form too vibrant and free to be confined to any strict following of rhyme, meter, and form.

William Wordsworth tried to define poetry as "the spontaneous overflow of powerful feelings…recollected in tranquility." However, if you have every tried to compose poetry, it is far from spontaneous, and even the best poets take years to refine their poems that have become classic today. The result of such creative outbursts of words on a blank page can be compared to some of the best works of art ever produced on canvas. Wordsworth's poem "Daffodils" can be compared with several of Claude Monet's paintings, especially "Field of Corn" (http://www.canvaz.com/gallery/754.htm) and "Tree" (http://www.canvaz.com/gallery/38.htm). In fact, Wordsworth said of this poem that it was his intention to bring the power and beauty of a poem to the middle and lower classes without it losing any merit. This poem could be displayed in a museum next to works of art by Monet and Van Gogh, for the enjoyment of art is not in the casual glancing of the picture but a long thoughtful study of the medium, and, in this sense, the words and how they create such a wondrous picture in our mind and a tranquil feeling in our soul.

Just as we started on a work of art, we will end with one as well. John Keats' "Ode on a Grecian Urn" praises a work of art that Keats probably viewed at an exhibition of Greek artifacts. In the same way the narrator praises the painted beauty of a woman in "My Last Duchess," Keats praises a lone Grecian urn as a mystery that is beyond any reason or explanation; this is what he coined "negative capability." What makes this ode seem so much richer than actually looking upon the Grecian urn itself is the rich use of language that pleases the ear. It is a poem meant to be spoken not read. Just as the urn he represents in the poem is a representation of classical Greek art, this poem, too, has been constructed at its purest, not merely as a vessel through which words flow, but as a receptacle of wonder and awe of an age now gone and only to be remembered through the words it represents. "Beauty is truth, truth beauty,"—that is all / Ye know on earth, and all ye need to know." Such fitting words to end this chapter, for words, like paint or stone, only have meaning when they represent beauty, not visually but mentally.

Robert Browning

My Last Duchess

Ferrara

That's my last Duchess painted on the wall,
Looking as if she were alive. I call
That piece a wonder, now: Frà Pandolf's hands
Worked busily a day, and there she stands.
Will't please you sit and look at her? I said
"Frà Pandolf" by design, for never read
Strangers like you that pictured countenance,
The depth and passion of its earnest glance,
But to myself they turned (since none puts by
The curtain I have drawn for you, but I)
And seemed as they would ask me, if they durst,
How such a glance came there; so, not the first
Are you to turn and ask thus. Sir, 'twas not
Her husband's presence only, called that spot
Of joy into the Duchess' cheek: perhaps
Frà Pandolf chanced to say, "Her mantle laps
Over my Lady's wrist too much," or "Paint
Must never hope to reproduce the faint
Half-flush that dies along her throat," such stuff
Was courtesy, she thought, and cause enough
For calling up that spot of joy. She had
A heart—how shall I say?—too soon made glad,
Too easily impressed; she liked whate'er
She looked on, and her looks went everywhere.

Sir, 'twas all one! My favor[1] at her breast,
The dropping of the daylight in the West,
The bough of cherries some officious fool
Broke in the orchard for her, the white mule
She rode with round the terrace—all and each
Would draw from her alike the approving speech,
Or blush, at least. She thanked men,—good ; but thanked
Somehow—I know not how—as if she ranked
My gift of a nine-hundred-years-old name
With anybody's gift. Who'd stoop to blame
This sort of trifling? Even had you skill
In speech—(which I have not)—to make your will
Quite clear to such an one, and say, "Just this
Or that in you disgusts me; here you miss,
Or there exceed the mark"—and if she let
Herself be lessoned so, nor plainly set
Her wits to yours, forsooth, and made excuse—
E 'en then would be some stooping; and I choose
Never to stoop. Oh, sir, she smiled, no doubt,
Whene'er I passed her; but who passed without
Much the same smile? This grew; I gave commands;
Then all smiles stopped together. There she stands
As if alive. Will 't please you rise? We'll meet
The company below, then. I repeat,
The Count your Master's known munificence
Is ample warrant that no just pretence
Of mine for dowry will be disallowed;
Though his fair daughter's self, as I avowed

---

[1] love token

At starting, is my object. Nay, we'll go
Together down, Sir! Notice Neptune, though,
Taming a sea-horse, thought a rarity,
Which Claus of Innsbruck cast in bronze for me.

Archibald Macleish

Ars Poetica

A poem should be palpable and mute
As a globed fruit,

Dumb
As old medallions to the thumb

Silent as the sleeve-worn stone
Of casement ledges where the moss has grown—

A poem should be wordless
As the flight of birds

A poem should be motionless in time
As the moon climbs,

Leaving, as the moon releases
Twig by twig the night-entangled trees,

Leaving, as the moon behind the winter leaves,
Memory by memory the mind—

A poem should be motionless in time
As the moon climbs.

A poem should be equal to:
Not true.

For all the history of grief
An empty doorway and a maple leaf.

For love,
The leaning grasses and two lights above the sea—

A poem should not mean
But be.

Marianne Moore

Poetry

I, too, dislike it: there are things that are important beyond all this fiddle.
    Reading it, however, with a perfect contempt for it, one discovers that there is in
    it after all, a place for the genuine.
        Hands that can grasp, eyes
        that can dilate, hair that can rise
            if it must, these things are important not because

a high-sounding interpretation can be put upon them but because they are
    useful; when they become so derivative as to become unintelligible,
the same thing may be said for all of us—that we
        do not admire what
        we cannot understand. The bat,
            holding on upside down or in quest of something

to eat, elephants pushing, a wild horse taking a roll, a tireless wolf under
    a tree, the immovable critic twitching his skin like a horse that feels a flea, the base-
    ball fan, the statistician—case after case
        could be cited did
        one wish it; nor is it valid
            to discriminate against "business documents and

school-books"; all these phenomena are important. One must make a distinction

however: when dragged into prominence by half poets, the result is not poetry,

nor till the poets among us can be

"literalists of

the imagination"—above

insolence and triviality and can present

for inspection, imaginary gardens with real toads in them, shall we have

it. In the meantime, if you demand on the one hand, in defiance of their opinion—

the raw material of poetry in

all its rawness and

that which is on the other hand,

genuine, you are interested in poetry.

William Wordsworth

Daffodils

I wandered lonely as a cloud
    That floats on high o'er vales and hills,
When all at once I saw a crowd,
    A host, of golden daffodils,
Beside the lake, beneath the trees,
Fluttering and dancing in the breeze.

Continuous as the stars that shine
    And twinkle on the milky way,
They stretched in never-ending line
    Along the margin of a bay:
Ten thousand saw I at a glance
Tossing their heads in sprightly dance.

The waves beside them danced, but they
    Out-did the sparkling waves in glee:--
A Poet could not but be gay
    In such a jocund company!
I gazed--and gazed--but little thought
What wealth the show to me had brought;

For oft, when on my couch I lie
    In vacant or in pensive mood,
They flash upon that inward eye
    Which is the bliss of solitude;
And then my heart with pleasure fills
And dances with the daffodils.

John Keats

Ode on a Grecian Urn

1

Thou still unravished bride of quietness,
    Thou foster-child of silence and slow time,
Sylvan historian, who canst thou express
    A flowery tale more sweetly than our rhyme:
What leaf-fringed legend haunt about thy shape
    Of deities or mortals, or of both,
        In Tempe or the dales of Arcady?
    What men or gods are these? What maidens loth?
What mad pursuit? What struggle to escape?
        What pipes and timbrels? What wild ecstasy?

2

Heard melodies are sweet, but those unheard
    Are sweeter: therefore, ye soft pipes, play on;
Not to the sensual ear, but, more endeared,
    Pipe to the spirit ditties of no tone:
Fair youth, beneath the trees, thou canst not leave
    Thy song, nor ever can those trees be bare;
        Bold lover, never, never canst thou kiss,
Though winning near the goal—yet, do not grieve;
        She cannot fade, though thou hast not thy bliss,
    For ever wilt thou love, and she be fair!

3

Ah, happy, happy boughs! that cannot shed

Your leaves, nor ever bid the spring adieu;
And, happy melodist, unweariè d,
For ever piping songs for ever new;
More happy love! more happy, happy love!
For ever warm and still to be enjoyed,
For ever panting, and for ever young;
All breathing human passion far above,
That leaves a heart high-sorrowful and cloyed,
A burning forehead, and a parching tongue.

4

Who are these coming to the sacrifice?
To what green altar, O mysterious priest,
Lead'st thou that heifer lowing at the skies,
And all her silken flanks with garlands dressed?
What little town by river or sea shore,
Or mountain-built with peaceful citadel,
Is emptied of this folk, this pious morn?
And, little town, thy streets for evermore
Will silent be; and not a soul to tell
Why thou art desolate, can e'er return.

5

O Attic shape! Fair attitude! with brede
Of marble men and maidens overwrought,
With forest branches and the trodden weed;
Thou, silent form, dost tease us out of thought
As doth eternity: Cold Pastoral!
When old age shall this generation waste,
Thou shalt remain, in midst of other woe

Than ours, a friend to man, to whom thou say'st,
"Beauty is truth, truth beauty,"—that is all
Ye know on earth, and all ye need to know.

Words & Phrases

adieu: goodbye.
ample: (adj) sufficient.
Arcady: (n) the poetic form of Arcadia, a mountain range in ancient Greece.
Attic: (adj) relating to Athens, Greece.
avowed: (adj) declared.
brede: (n) something braided. No longer used.
casement: (n) a window that opens outward on hinges.
cloy: (v) to be weary of pleasure.
derivative: (adj) secondary; unoriginal.
dilate: (v) to become larger.
ditties: (n) poems that are sung; plural of ditty.
dost: (v) old form of does.
dowry: (n) money that the bride's family gives to the groom.
durst: (v) old form of dared.
flank: (n) the side of the animal between the ribs and back leg.
forsooth: (adv) old form of in truth.
Fra: (n) a friar in the Roman Catholic Church.
garland: (n) a wreath of flowers.
heifer: (n) a young cow.
jocund: (adj) cheerful.
lap: (v) to hang over.
loth: (adj) unwilling.
low: (v) moo. The sound a cow makes.
mantle: (n) a cape or cloak.
milky way: (n) a band of stars in the sky that makes up the arm of our galaxy; it looks like a "milky" road in the

sky.

munificence: (n) generosity.

Neptune: (n) Roman god of the Sea. Poseidon is the Greek name.

officious: (adj) eager to serve.

palpable: (adj) easily felt by the five senses.

pensive: (adj) thoughtful.

sprightly: (adv) to move in a lively way.

stoop: (v) to yield or submit to another.

sylvan: (adj) a person or thing that lives in the woods.

Tempe: (n) a valley in E Greece.

timbrel: (n) a tambourine.

triviality: (n) something of little importance.

unravished: (adj) virgin.

warrant: (n) guarantee

Study Questions

1. Poets before the Romantic Period (late 18th to early 19th century) were very strict with their rhymes. They follow a set formula. During the Romantic Period, poets started to experiment more with other various rhymes to create diversity in their verse. A slant rhyme is the opposite of the exact rhyme. Slant rhymes use the same final consonants while the vowels differ, while exact rhymes use the sounds following the vowel as the same. Some examples of a slant rhymes for go**d** are moo**d**, mo**d**e, ma**d**e, gree**d**, fa**d**. While the exact rhymes of g**od** are s**od**, r**od**, o**dd**, l**aud**. There are many examples of slant rhymes in this volume, but John Keats used many of them in his "Ode on a Grecian Urn." Can you spot the slant rhymes? What are they?

2. Perhaps you noticed some words that have the same spelling but different sounds. Are these slant rhymes, too? No. They are eye rhymes (i.e. said and raid; lush and push). Can you spot the eye rhymes in the same poem?

3. Browning's "My Last Duchess" is an example of a poetical dramatic monologue. Here the reader understands a certain situation through the Duke's point of view. Reread the poem. Who is the poem about, the Duchess or the Duke? If we break this poem into three parts, the first part (lines 1-13) is the Duke speaking about the portrait of his wife. She is a beautiful woman and Fra Pandolf painted her portrait. What can we learn about the Duchess from these initial lines? What about the Duke?

4. The second part (13-46) reveals more about the Duke. What does the Duke mean when he says, "Sir, twas not / her husband's presence only, called that spot / Of joy into the Duchess cheek"? Connect his line with, "She had / a heart ... how shall I say? ... too soon made glad, / Too easily impressed; she liked whate'er / She looked on, and her looks went everywhere." What can we deduce the Duchess has done? Can we believe the Duke in what he says of his wife? Why or why not? This next line perhaps sums up the Duke's pride and mistrust, "She thanked men, --good; but thanked / Somehow ... I know not how ... as if she ranked / My gift of a nine-hundred year old name / With anybody's gift."

5. The Duke also says, "I gave commands; / Then all smiles stopped together. There she stands / As if alive." What did the Duke do? What were his commands? How did her smiles stop? How can you know this is what happened?

6. The third part (46-56) shows why the Duke is a Duke. He is the master of diplomacy and turns quickly from a personal confession to the business at hand by reminding his listener who he really is, and how high he is in society. He is merely boasting to one of lesser status. How do you feel about the Duke now that you have read the poem? Explain your answer.

7. Remember that a dramatic dialogue is heard only through the voice of a character, as if listening to a person

talk on the telephone. The idea is to use a point of view different from your own. Browning was neither domineering of women or a murderer, yet that is the voice he took in "My Last Duchess." Reread Keats' "Ode on a Grecian Urn." Could this be considered a dramatic dialogue? Why or why not? Do you think this is really Keats talking, or is it some other character?

8. Compare Macleish's poem with Moore's. How do they feel about poetry? Do they feel the same way? Explain with examples from the poem.

9. Compare Wordsworth's poem "Daffodils" with the paintings of similar theme (see Claude Monet's "Field of Corn" http://www.canvaz.com/gallery/754.htm and "Tree" http://www. canvaz.com/gallery/38.htm). Which do you find a better representation of the scene, the poem or the picture? Explain.

10. Can poetry be just as descriptive as art? Explain. Can it be better than art? Explain. In what ways can the written word be better than a picture or painting?

11. What is your favorite poem on art? Why is it your favorite?

X. THEME TEN: CONCRETE POEMS

Introduction
Poetic Texts
Words & Phrases
Study Questions

INTRODUCTION TO THEME TEN

Concrete Poems

A parallel with our poems on art are concrete poems, poems that rely upon the visual as much as the use of words. In other words, the only content of the poem is to convey a certain picture in the mind of the reader either visually, as in setting words of the poems into an actual picture (George Herbert's "Easter Wings") or in using minimal words to portray a single object in time (Ezra Pound's "In a Station in a Metro").

George Herbert's "Easter Wings" is probably the most famous and anthologized concrete poem. Not only is it written to look like the wings of an angel, but the poem is a prayer offered up to God that both literally and figuratively rises to heaven. This is the type of poem that offers not only an aesthetic quality visually but also orally. "The Altar" is another example of the image representing the poem, this time a weatherworn and cracked altar used as a prayer to the Lord. Both poems appeared in a collection of works called *The Temple* and published after George Herbert, a minister, asked them to be published upon his death. The visual image of the altar is interesting to note, for he showcases four words in all capital letters: altar, heart, sacrifice, and altar again. The representation to meaning is obvious. The narrator is placing his heart on top of the altar as a sacrifice to the Lord. The fact that they are capitalized "breaks" the rhythm of the visual, and they appear as cracks on the altar itself. *The Temple*, in fact, reads like walking through a grand cathedral, where the first poem begins on the church porch, continues into the church, comments on stained windows as well as the people who come to worship and the themes preached within.

In the same vein as Herbert's visual poetry is Lewis Carroll's (1832-1898) "The Mouse's Tail," which is featured in *Alice's Adventure in Wonderland.* Obvious is the relation of the image of a mouse's tail to the actual tale the mouse was speaking of. Interesting to note, though, is the quadruple pun of the word "tale." First are the two obvious meanings of tale/tail, as in story and the tail of the mouse. The third pun is the tail-rhyme used in the actual poem. A tail-rhyme, or end rhyme, has two words that rhyme at the end of two short sentences followed by a longer sentence that does not rhyme. For example, "Fury said to a mouse, / That he met in a house, 'Let us both go to law: I will prosecute you.'" Here we can see two short sentences that rhyme followed by a longer one that does not. When the poem is written with a tail rhyme in mind, instead of traditionally, it actually forms the mouse's tail, which is why Carroll chose to write his poem in this fashion. The fourth pun is in the actual organization of the line with two short lines followed by a longer line, which reminds us of a a mouse's tail.

Since many concrete poems were written in the past sixty years and are still under copyright, it is difficult to get differing examples. I have included one of my own experiments here just to show another example of the relation of image to the word. The title "Uroboros" relates to the ancient symbol of the serpent eating its own tail, forming a complete circle. It carries the meaning of eternity, but a cyclical one with a continuous beginning and end. The image of the sonnet, like the serpent the poem tries to represent, is circular, and where it ends, it all begins again. It is like a poem that is not meant to end, but encourages the reader to continue on reading for all eternity.

The second style of concrete poetry is the imagist style, where minimal words are used to "photograph" a certain scene, freezing it in time. The art or skill comes from the poet being able to capture the nature of that scene in as few words as possible. Ezra Pound's (1885-1972) "In a Station in the Metro" was his attempt to capture an experience he had in a Paris subway where, upon exiting the train, he noticed faces that were beautiful to behold. He suffered for a year over the image, trying to put into words what he experienced. He went from a thirty line poem to a fifteen line poem and destroyed both knowing that they did not capture the portrait-like event that he had experienced. What he decided upon is best put in his own words, "In a poem of this sort one is trying to record the precise instant when a thing outward and objective transforms itself, or darts into a thing inward a subjective.[1]" When he finished, he managed to create a photogenic piece of poetry.

Of similar mind is Carl Sandburg's (1878-1967) "Fog." As Pound's previous poem captures a snapshot moment in time, so, too, does "Fog." However, Sandburg's poem is

---

1 See http://rpo.library.utoronto.ca/poem/1657.html

quite active and is able to capture a still moment by infusing it with motion. Just as if we were to sit and watch the fog roll into the harbor, we would barely notice the motion. We would sit and watch the fog stretch out before us, and before we knew it, we would be surrounded by it, and then it would be gone. Sandburg's imagist poem is perfection in the art of motion through static observation.

George Herbert

Easter Wings

Lord, who createdst man in wealth and store,
Though foolishly he lost the same,
Decaying more and more,
Till he became
Most poor:
With thee
Oh let me rise
As larks, harmoniously,
And sing this day thy victories:
Then shall the fall further the flight in me.

My tender age in sorrow did begin:
And still with sicknesses and shame
Thou didst so punish sin,
That I became
Most thin.
With thee
Let me combine
And feel this day thy victory:
For, if I imp my wing on thine
Affliction shall advance the flight in me.

George Herbert

The Altar

A broken ALTAR, Lord thy servant rears,
Made of a heart, and cemented with tears:
Whose parts are as thy hand did frame;
No workman's tool hath touched the same
A HEART alone
Is such a stone,
As nothing but
Thy power doth cut.
Wherefore each part
Of my hard heart
Meets in this frame,
To praise thy Name:
That if I chance to hold my peace,
These stones to praise thee may not cease.
O let thy blessed SACRIFICE be mine,
And sanctify this ALTAR to be thine.

Lewis Carroll

The Mouse's Tail

"Mine is a long and a sad tale!" said the Mouse, turning to Alice, and sighing. "It *is* a long tail, certainly," said Alice, looking down with wonder at the Mouse's tail; "but why do you call it sad?" And she kept on puzzling about it while the Mouse was speaking, so that her idea of the tale was something like this:—"

Fury said to a mouse,
That he met in the
house, 'Let us
both go to law:
I will prosecute
you.-- Come, I'll
take no denial;
We must have
a trial: For
really this
morning I've
nothing to do.'
Said the mouse
to the cur,
'Such a trial,
dear Sir, With
no jury or
judge, would
be wasting
our breath.'
'I'll be
judge, I'll
be jury,'
Said cunning
old Fury:
'I'll try
the whole
cause, and
condemn
you
to
death.'

Steven Reeder

Uroboros

ETE
It all begins again……. **L CIRCLE,**
in the end   **RNA**   never
pain, **For**   ending
With no   time
wholeness   **Thy**
boundless   strands
that   unwind
To seal   and then
gone,   divide.
and   **Thou**
is dead   snake,
what   upon
on   whose
devour,   back
So bite,   eons decline;
to last.   **Thy head,**
seems   man's birth
nothing   bears
the future,   tooth'd
on **Towards**   maw
and stumble   gaping wide
to rush   **Towards** thy
mankind   tail, where
To cause   dead damnation
the past,   waits **Towards**
headlong into   that end where
The present falls   generations spin
beneath the skin.   Down centuries of time
Now, all that was stagnates,   so full of hate.

Ezra Pound

In a Station in the Metro

The apparition of these faces in the crowd;
Petals on a wet, black bough.

Carl Sandburg

Fog

The fog comes
on little cat feet.

It sits looking
over harbor and city
on silent haunches
and then moves on

Words & Phrases

apparition: (n) appearance.
cur: (n) a mean person.
eon: (n) an uncountable period of time.
haunches: (n) the back part and legs of animals.
imp: (v) insert; graft.
maw: (n) mouth.
rear: (v) to build.
store: (n) supplies of food, clothes, and other household necessities.
Uroboros: (n) a snake or dragon forming a circle eating its tail; represents infinity.

Study Questions

1. "Feature verse" is writing a poem in the shape of the topic. Herbert's examples are probably the best. Do you like these kinds of poems? Do they add to or distract from the beauty of the written word? Explain.

2. Do you know any other feature verse not included in this text? Which is your favorite?

3. Try writing your own concrete poem on a common subject.

4. Ezra Pound's poem is very short, only two lines. Can this really be considered a poem? Why or why not? How is it effective?

5. What do you think Carroll is trying to say in "The Mouse's Tail"?

6. What is the poet in "Uroboros" trying to say? How is time like a serpent devouring its tail?

7. How does the picture form of the poem help with meaning behind the word? Use examples from the poem.

8. How do concrete poems parallel art poems? Use examples from the poems.

XI. THEME ELEVEN: CHRISTIAN THEMES

Introduction

Poetic Texts

Words & Phrases

Study Questions

INTRODUCTION TO THEME ELVEVEN

Christian Themes

Since the focus of our study is America and Britain, it is natural that the poetry would reflect the predominant religion, Christianity. While most poets found Biblical symbolism aesthetically pleasing, others turned to allegory to go even deeper into the Christian themes they were working with. Allegory, while similar to a metaphor, extends further than a mere symbol that fits within the narrative and goes outside the narrative as a whole different story. It is a story that wears the present story as a mask to hide its intent or meaning from others who would not understand. Most of the words and ideas contain at least two meanings. An example of an allegory from the Bible is Jonah and the whale. Jonah is swallowed by the whale and spends three days in its belly before being belched onto the beach safely. This is an allegory of Christ dying, spending three days in death, and returning through resurrection. Thus, allegory was often used as a way to both criticize and praise Christian ideals without the poet ever appearing dangerous to the ruling Church or preachy to the reader.

William Blake lived in a time of political and religious strife. He believed in the equality of the human spirit, which meant that he was against slavery and equality of the sexes, both of which the Church of England were not known to favor. Blake may often appear as anti-religious, but his poetry, when read as an allegory, shows he was deeply religious and knew the Bible well. "The Lamb" and "The Tyger" are two poems that show Blake's differing views on religion. "The Lamb" comes from a collection called *Songs of Innocence*, which expresses an almost innocent, childish view the religious hold over their faith. It is a poem that speaks of Christ and compares his life with the like of a little lamb. The simplicity of the language, rhythm and rhyme also enforces the simplicity of innocence. "The Tyger" comes from a later collection called *Songs of Experience*, which expresses his opinion that children lost their innocence by being exploited by religion that casts aside mercy in favor of dogma. Blake was not against experience, he just felt that children should gain experience in a natural way and find God and the world on their own without any religious bias. Most of the poems in *Experience* parallel *Innocence*. "The Tyger" was meant to mirror "The Lamb" and even references the lamb by saying, "Did he who made the Lamb make thee?" The lamb is symbolic of innocence and frailty, a perfect metaphor for Christ, who was slaughtered like a lamb. The tiger, then, is Blake's metaphor for God, who created death and suffering. The question raised is how could a God who created the bright and happy Lamb (mercy) have created the dark and gloomy Tiger (law and judgment). Here creation is viewed as dark, where life is not always one of joy. Contrasted against "The Lamb," which is childish, "The Tyger" expresses an adult's wearier outlook on the world. The point being, we cannot have one state of existence without the other. Blake firmly believed in progression through opposition. One must be innocent before encountering harsh experiences, which allow one to reach a higher level of understanding about the world. Only then could one understand the true role of religion, for what does a saint need of religion if he or she is already perfect?

W.B. Yeats had a somewhat darker approach to religion than Blake. With Blake there was hope. Even though Blake had lost hope for humanity after the French Revolution turned from individualism back to an empire, he knew there was a purpose to everything that all of humanity needed in order to gain experience. For Yeats, he had lost all hope for his Age. Being Irish, he was disenchanted by British colonial rule and witnessed the blatant destruction and horror of World War I. For Yeats, in "The Second Coming," the ideals of Christianity were well on their way out as a falcon continues to circle wider and wider, having lost sight of its master until entirely lost. The first stanza speaks of the way the narrator views the world, a world of anarchy and loss of innocence. The second stanza intones the need for revelation, the much anticipated Second Coming of Christ, perhaps. However, as all things in the past, the old must give way to the new. The *Spiritus Mundi* that he sees is the soul of the world has taken on the shape of a horrible sphinx, "A shape with lion body and the head of a man," and instead of the promised light of the world coming, darkness and shadows follow. Just as the dove announced the birth of a Christian age, desert birds, buzzards most likely for they feed on death, announce the opening of this new age that, for Yeats, drew to an end after World War I. Instead of the Christ child born in the manger "twenty centuries" ago, a new "Messiah" now

"Slouches towards Bethlehem to be born." What this beast was to be, we may never know. Thank goodness Yeats wasn't speaking prophetically but allegorically. We get a sense of nihilism that was common during this age of depression and war, where many had lost hope in religion to bring them out of the darkness and turned, instead, to despair.

While despair and abandonment may be the only way to look at the world as it is today, the religious still try and deal with their own role in life. John Milton's "When I Consider How My Light is Spent" offers a conversation between the narrator and God. The first octet of the poem is the speaker questioning how God will judge him. The reference to the one talent that he couldn't hide but did nothing with directly brings to mind Jesus' parable of the talents, where God gives us varying skills and blesses those who do the best of their ability with the skills God has given them; God curses those who hide their talent and scoffs at those who use their talent for overabundance. In this poem, the narrator feels God will curse him for hiding his own talent. He asks a rhetorical question about God being a task master and demanding work in exchange for "light" or spiritual illumination. The sestet that follows is God's unexpected response through the man's conscience. God reminds us that he does not require work nor need it but requires those who are willing to serve him with an open heart. It is not what we do; it is how we do it. He then gently reminds the narrator that God is like a king with thousands of angels to do as he asks, so it is not for man to worry about doing things for God; God has it taken care of. What God does ask for is faith in God, while all that is at God's disposal is at the faithfuls' as well.

How is one to read John Donne's "Holy Sonnet 14"? Not only is the narrator asking God to "batter" him but to also rape him! There is a fine line between the divine and the profane in this poem, and Donne manages to erase it with his metaphors. The previous poets have shown that they fear God; Donne shows us that God is not to be feared. The only way to understand God, and when Donne says God, he means Jesus as part of the "three-personed God" (the Holy Trinity), and what he wants from us is to give ourselves over to him. The path of a "saint" is not an easy way. By being human we are married to the enemy, the Devil, and must be shown that it is not actually God who makes us suffer so, but ourselves, who so choose to go down a different path of experience only to discover that is not the way we want to go. The only way to make it to the right place is if God reminds us, who are "weak and untrue," with strict laws and commandments that "break, blow, burn, and make me new." The same rational is applied to a man who, through error, lights himself on fire. To throw water on him and roll him in the dirt will obviously be painful, but, in the end, to his advantage and salvation.

The poets in this chapter will be the first to tell you that those who follow God are far from perfect. If any proclaim they are perfect, they are probably lying to themselves. George Herbert, who was a minister, found it hard to be a responsible leader of a flock of sinners while he too was a sinner, for ministers are human and, therefore, sin. The narrator in “The Collar” is also a minister who strikes the board of his table set with meat and fruit. It would appear that the minister is in prayer and ends it by striking the table with finality. He is tired and wishes for something better than a poor life of a minister. He complains that God has given him nothing but misery for faithful service, a thorn instead of fruit. The corn and wine of the sacrament he sees only as temporal rewards—he has forgotten the eternal significance of these emblems. He plans on a life of pleasure before he is too old. He calls his service to God a cage and God’s law as shackles. While he raves and grows “more fierce and wild,” he hears the still, small voice of God call out, “Child!” He responds, “My Lord.” Such a poem juxtaposes the feelings of our heart, which Donne wishes God to beat out in our last poem, with the feelings of our mind. There is a sense in the poem that the narrator becomes child-like, in that when we stray, no matter how far and rebelliously, God will be there to bring us back with a soft word, and we will be eternally thankful for that.

William Blake

The Lamb

Little Lamb who made thee?
Dost thou know who made thee?
Gave thee life & bid thee feed,
By the stream & o'er the mead;
Gave thee clothing of delight,
Softest clothing wooly bright;
Gave thee such a tender voice,
Making all the vales rejoice!
Little Lamb who made thee?
Dost thou know who made thee?

Little Lamb I'll tell thee,
Little Lamb I'll tell thee!
He is callèd by thy name,
For he calls himself a Lamb:
He is meek & he is mild,
He became a little child:
I a child & thou a lamb,
We are called by his name.
Little Lamb God bless thee.
Little Lamb God bless thee.

William Blake

The Tyger

Tyger! Tyger! burning bright
In the forests of the night,
What immortal hand or eye
Could frame thy fearful symmetry?

In what distant deeps or skies
Burnt the fire of thine eyes?
On what wings dare he aspire?
What the hand, dare seize the fire?

And what shoulder, & what art,
Could twist the sinews of thy heart?
And when thy heart began to beat,
What dread hand? & what dread feet?

What the hammer? what the chain,
In what furnace was thy brain?
What the anvil? what dread grasp
Dare its deadly terrors clasp?

When the stars threw down their spears[1],
And watered heaven with their tears,
Did he smile his work to see?
Did he who made the Lamb make thee?

---

[1] the third host of heaven that was cast out with Lucifer after the War in Heaven. See Revelations 12:7-10.

Tyger! Tyger! burning bright
In the forests of the night,
What immortal hand or eye
Dare frame thy fearful symmetry?

W.B. Yeats

The Second Coming

Turning and turning in the widening gyre
The falcon cannot hear the falconer;
Things fall apart; the center cannot hold;
Mere anarchy is loosed upon the world,
The blood-dimmed tide is loosed, and everywhere
The ceremony of innocence is drowned;
The best lack all conviction, while the worst
Are full of passionate intensity.

Surely some revelation is at hand;
Surely the Second Coming is at hand.
The Second Coming! Hardly are those words out
When a vast image out of *Spritus Mundi*
Troubles my sight: somewhere in sands of the desert
A shape with lion body and the head of a man[2],
A gaze blank and pitiless as the sun,
Is moving its slow thighs, while all about it
Reel shadows of the indignant desert birds.
The darkness drops again; but now I know
That twenty centuries of stony sleep
were vexed to nightmare by a rocking cradle,
And what rough beast, its hour come round at last,
Slouches towards Bethlehem to be born?

---

2 A sphinx

John Milton

When I Consider How My Light is Spent

When I consider how my light is spent
Ere half my days in this dark world and wide,
And that one talent which is death to hide
Lodged with me useless, though my soul more bent
To serve therewith my Maker, and present
My true account, lest he returning chide,
"Doth God exact day-labor, light denied?"
I fondly ask. But Patience, to prevent
That murmur, soon replies: "God doth not need
Either man's work or his own gifts: who best
Bear his mild yoke, they serve him best. His state
Is kingly; Thousands at his bidding speed
And post o'er land and ocean without rest:
They also serve who only stand and wait."

John Donne

Holy Sonnet 14

Batter my heart, three-personed God[3]; for You
As yet but knock breathe, shine, and seek to mend;
That I may rise and stand, o'erthrow me, and bend
Your force to break, blow, burn, and make me new.
I, like an usurped town, to another due,
Labor to admit You, but O, to no end,
Reason, Your viceroy in me, me should defend,
But is captived, and proves weak or untrue.
Yet dearly I love You, and would be loved fain,
But am betrothed unto your enemy[4].
Divorce me, untie or break that knot again,
Take me to You, imprison me, for I,
Except You enthrall me, never shall be free,
Nor ever chaste, except You ravish me.

---

3 The Trinity; God the Father, Jesus the Son, and the Holy Spirit.

4 The Devil; Satan.

George Herbert

The Collar

I struck the board and cried, "No more,
I will abroad!
What? shall I ever sigh and pine?
My lines and life are free, free as the road,
Loose as the wind, as large as store.
Shall I be still in suit?
Have I no harvest but a thorn
To let me blood, and not restore
What I have lost with cordial fruit?
Sure there was wine
Before my sighs did dry it, there was corn
Before my tears did drown it.
Is the year only lost to me?
Have I no bays to crown it,
No flowers, no garlands gay? all blasted?
All wasted?
Not so, my heart: but there is fruit,
And thou hast hands.
Recover all thy sigh-blown age
On double pleasures: leave thy cold dispute
Of what is fit and not. Forsake thy cage,
Thy rope of sands,
Which petty thoughts have made, and made to thee
Good cable, to enforce and draw,
And be thy law,
While thou didst wink and wouldst not see.

Away! take heed:
I will abroad.
Call in thy death's-head there; tie up thy fears.
He that forbears
To suit and serve his need,
Deserves his load."
But as I raved and grew more fierce and wild
At every word,
Me thoughts I heard one calling, *Child!*
And I replied, *My Lord.*

Words & Phrases

aspire: (v) rise up.
bay: (n) a wreath of leaves; laurel.
betrothed: (adj) to be engaged.
bid: (v) command.
board: (n) table.
chide: (v) scold.
conviction: (n) firm belief.
cordial: (adj) life-giving.
deaths-head: (n) a skull; symbolizes mortality.
enthrall: (v) enslave.
fain: (adv) willingly.
gyre: (n) spiral.
knot: (n) marriage not.
Maker: (n) God.
mead: (n) meadow.
pine: (v) regret or yearn.
post: (v) to announce publicly.
ravish: (v) to violate or rape.
reel: (v) to move in a circular pattern.
Second Coming: (n) the return of Jesus Christ at the end of days to save the righteous from the wicked.
sinew: (n) muscle; probably meant as strength here.
Spiritus Mundi: Latin for Spirit of the World.
store: (n) abundance.
suit: (adj) asking favors.
symmetry: (n) shape.
usurp: (v) to take control of something by force.
vex: (v) to torment.

viceroy: (n) a person appointed to rule.
yoke: (n) a wooden frame that joins two animals together; a symbol of subjection.

Study Questions

1. A popular stanza style for lyrical poetry is the quatrain. A quatrain is a stanza of four lines that usually contains the rhyme scheme of *aabb, abab,* or *aaba*. If you look throughout this collection of poetry, it is not difficult to spot quatrain poems. In Blake's *Songs of Innocence* and *Songs of Experience*, 36 of his 46 poems utilize the quatrain.

Reread "The Lamb" and "The Tyger." Thematically both poems are the same; the Lamb represents the soul of innocence, or a child, whereas the Tyger represents the soul of an adult changed by the world. What style differences do you see between these two poems? How does the use of the quatrain change the effect of "The Tyger"?

2. Look at the first quatrain in Blake's "The Tyger." Notice the rhyme of "eye" and "symmetry." Are these exact rhymes? Do we have to read "symmetry" with the same rhyme ending as "eye"? This device is called an imperfect or an approximate rhyme, used more and more by modern poets. Can you find any other approximate rhymes in this volume? Does it hurt the overall texture of the poem? Do you think it perhaps emphasizes certain points the poet wants to make? Or couldn't he/she find a better word to rhyme? Explain.

3. If "The Lamb" is about Christ, then is it fair to say that "The Tyger" is about the Devil? Why not? Reread "The Tyger." Notice the questions and language used. What

does this have to say about the creator of the tiger? Is the creator of the tiger really the same as the creator of the lamb? Explain such a contradiction?

4. Most poems contain symbols, an object or representation that implies additional meaning beyond its own. Does this mean we can add any symbol we want to the object or idea? It would no longer be a symbol if we did. The power of the poem is the poet's ability to guide the reader into the very essence of the symbol. W.B. Yeats takes a well known symbol and flips it. Reread "The Second Coming." What Second Coming does he refer to? Read carefully. Can it be the Second Coming of Christ? Why or why not?

5. Remember that "Second Coming" was written in the aftermath of World War I. Thus, with the end of the world, who will appear in "a shape with lion body and head of a man, / A gaze blank and pitiless as the sun"?

6. Why does Yeats reference the Sphinx myth in this poem?

7. Can "The Second Coming" be considered a Christian poem? Why or why not?

8. In Milton's poem, there is strife in the narrator's soul. What is the resolution at the end of the poem?

9. Why does the narrator of Donne's Holy Sonnet feel the need to have God be so rough with him? What is the

juxtaposition between the first twelve lines and the final couplet?

10. A pun is a play on words that sound the same but carry different meanings. George Herbert's title is a double pun. Explain the double pun in context of the poem. Use examples from the poem in your answer.

11. Why is it that the narrator of "The Collar" is so belligerent before God and then in the final two lines is so subservient? Explain this seemingly contradictory turn of events in the poem? Is it really so contradictory?

X. THEME TWELVE: **FREEDOM**

Introduction

Poetic Texts

Words & Phrases

Study Questions

INTRODUCTION TO THEME TWELVE

Freedom

Freedom has various contexts, but we will look at how our featured poets view freedom as both an internal and external desire. As far as having internal freedom, many would think of self-reliance, others would equate spiritual freedom as well, including inner peace, self control, and a sense of free will. With external freedom, ideas of not being dominated by another or having a government that upholds general liberties usually come to mind. Rebellion and revolution are cries for freedom from a suppressed state. Freedom is often equated with happiness, and it parallels our Christian themes because religious freedom often leads to freedom of the soul from the bondage of sin or guilt.

Percy Bysshe Shelley's "Ode to the West Wind" deals with internal freedom and the wish to move that freedom outward to bring change in others. Sections I through III deal with how the wind influences the earth, wind, and water. There is a sense of freedom in how Shelley alliteratively describes the "wild West Wind," and its ability to go anywhere and do as it pleases. Section IV deals with the narrator asking the wind for its power of movement since he, as an earthbound man, can hardly do what he wishes. Section V has the narrator asking the wind to be his own spirit, or muse as it were, and take his ideas of "dead thoughts" like dead leaves and spread them throughout the world. As a poet, the narrator feels free in thought and imagination but stuck upon the earth without any way of letting the world know his thoughts. The wind could serve as "The trumpet of a prophecy," to bring about a change in humanity. If the world is tired and dead in the wintry grip of tyrants and kings, perhaps with his words blowing through the wind, spring is not too far off.

As much as Shelley's poem speaks of internal freedom William Blake championed external freedom in what he saw as a bleak, dark age. As one of the forerunners of the Romantic Period, Blake was concerned with the abolishment of slaves, the rights of women, and the abuse of the poor by the wealthy. In "London," Blake concentrates on the problems of personal freedom and social justice in the London of his time. In sharp contrast to the pastoral images in his Songs of Innocence, Blake opens his poem with the image of every street and even the mighty river Thames being chartered, being partitioned to ownership by some lord or owner. Nothing in London is free or natural. On top of that we have restricting laws, a religion that is no longer pure ("black'ning church appalls"), excessive poverty, and starving children that leads to more crime and suffering such as disease and prostitution. Notice that none of the people he talks about are seen; they are only heard through their sighs or cries or have left traces of blood. This is the world of experience for Blake and any talk of freedom is but a laughable expression as long as religious authorities and the upper class turn a blind eye to the situation.

Blake also introduces the chimney sweeper that later makes a personal appearance in "The Chimney Sweeper."

This poem addresses more intimately the idea of slavery, especially child labor. The idea of a child being sold because of poverty was and still is a reality in almost all cultures. What is disturbing in this poem is the use of religion to placate the child to feel he is doing his duty. On first reading, it would seem that religion actually helps the child survive in the dark and dreary world that has been forced upon him and actually brings joy where there is none. But if you understand Blake's disdain of the religious institutions of his day while being a deeply religious man, you start to see this poem in a different light. Compare this with the operation of suicide bombers and the joy they feel when killing themselves and other's. The only way to get someone to do their duty and not complain and try to change their station in life, according to Blake, is to placate them into accepting their fate. In this poem, religion is used to keep the boy in line and working as a slave. The last line is rather chilling, "So if all do their duty they need not fear harm." Be a good sheep and you will not be harmed. Doing something to avoid harm is far from being free and is probably the worst reality of most "civilized" societies.

Lord Gordon Byron (1788-1824), as well, had great disdain for social institutions that refused to reform or allow personal freedoms to all classes. He even went to Greece to fight with the Greek insurgency for independence from the Ottoman Empire. He used his own funds to arm Greek soldiers under him and, though he wasn't a soldier, would fight with them. Unfortunately, he grew sick before he could leave and eventually died from his sickness.

However, his works captured his spirit to such a degree that most of his characters bear his name as Byronic heroes. Such heroes show dislike for social institutions and accompanying rank and privileges. They often rebel and then suffer exile, while their great talent and passion helps to bring about self-destruction. Though it is but a sonnet, "The Sonnet of Chillon" features an actual person that is an ideal Byronic hero; thus, this character's life drew Byron to his story like a magnet. Chillon is a castle on the shore of Lake Geneva in Switzerland that once held a Genovois monk, Francois Bonivard, from 1532 to 1536. At a young age, Francois opposed Charles III, the Duke of Savoy, from taking control of Geneva. For his rebellious efforts, Bonivard was imprisoned for three years. Upon his release, he continued his rebellion. He was imprisoned yet again for 6 years in Chillon, "brightest of dungeons." He was freed after the fall of the Duke. Obviously, Byron felt such characters who upheld others' freedoms over their own were worthy of praise.

Our last poet, Anna Laetitia Barbauld (1743-1825), speaks of freedom for women's rights, an idea that still is being expanded to this day. In her poem "The Rights of Women," she shows her ideas of women's rights in light of the feminist movement of her day. Though this poem lacks poetic metaphors, it is full of irony. First and foremost, it is an attack on Mary Wollstonecraft's *Vindication of the Rights of Women* (1792) and must be read as ironic. If the poem seems over militant, it is. Barbauld felt that the rights of women should not be a reversal of what women had already suffered under. Irony is clear in such lines: "Go, bid proud Man his boasted rule resign / And kiss the golden scepter of thy reign," and "Make treacherous Man thy subject, not thy friend, / Thou mayst command, but never canst be free." These lines are clearly mocking Wollstonecraft's stance against women's use of sensibility because they fall victim to their senses. It was Wollstonecraft's attack against Barbauld's idea of sensibility that led Barbauld to attack back by showing women acting without sensibility. What Wollstonecraft saw as freeing women from the "evils" of masculine imposed roles on women, Barbauld saw as destructive to the women's cause. Women are only free when "mutual love" is achieved by both sexes.

This brings us, once again, full circle to our very first topic, Love. Love is what actually frees all humanity and creates understanding. It is a cure for all the negative ideas discussed in our various themes and a companion of all the positive ones. Thus ends our twelve topics on poetry, start again and see old ideas in a new light.

Percy Bysshe Shelley

Ode to the West Wind

O wild West Wind, thou breath of Autumn's being,
Thou, from whose unseen presence the leaves dead
Are driven, like ghosts from an enchanter fleeing,

Yellow, and black, and pale, and hectic red,
Pestilence-stricken multitudes: O thou,
Who chariotest to their dark wintry bed

The wingèd seeds, where they lie cold and low,
Each like a corpse within its grave, until
Thine azure sister of the Spring shall blow

Her clarion o'er the dreaming earth, and fill
(Driving sweet buds like flocks to feed in air)
With living hues and odors plain and hill:

Wild Spirit, which art moving everywhere;
Destroyer and preserver; hear, oh, hear!

II

Thou on whose stream, mid the steep skys commotion,
Loose clouds like earth's decaying leaves are shed,
Shook from the tangled boughs of Heaven and Ocean,

Angels of rain and lightning: there are spread
On the blue surface of thine aery surge,

Like the bright hair uplifted from the head

Of some fierce Maenad, even from the dim verge
Of the horizon to the zenith's height,
The locks of the approaching storm. Thou dirge

Of the dying year, to which this closing night
Will be the dome of a vast sepulcher,
Vaulted with all thy congregated might

Of vapors, from whose solid atmosphere
Black rain, and fire, and hail will burst: oh, hear!

III

Thou who didst waken from his summer dreams
The blue Mediterranean, where he lay,
Lulled by the coil of his crystalline streams,

Beside a pumice isle in Baiae's bay,
And saw in sleep old palaces and towers
Quivering within the wave's intenser day,

All overgrown with azure moss and flowers
So sweet, the sense faints picturing them! Thou
For whose path the Atlantic's level powers

Cleave themselves into chasms, while far below
The sea-blooms and the oozy woods which wear
The sapless foliage of the ocean know

Thy voice, and suddenly grow gray with fear,
And tremble and despoil themselves: oh, hear!

IV

If I were a dead leaf thou mightest bear;
If I were a swift cloud to fly with thee;
A wave to pant beneath thy power, and share

The impulse of thy strength, only less free
Than thou, O uncontrollable! If even
I were as in my boyhood, and could be

The comrade of thy wanderings over Heaven,
As then, when to outstrip thy skiey speed
Scarce seemed a vision; I would ne'er have striven

As thus with thee in prayer in my sore need.
Oh, lift me as a wave, a leaf, a cloud!
I fall upon the thorns of life! I bleed!

A heavy weight of hours has chained and bowed
One too like thee: tameless, and swift and proud.

V

Make me thy lyre, even as the forest is:
What if my leaves are falling like its own!
The tumult of thy mighty harmonies

Will take from both a deep, autumnal tone,
Sweet though in sadness. Be thou, Spirit fierce,

My spirit! Be thou me, impetuous one!

Drive my dead thoughts over the universe
Like withered leaves to quicken a new birth!
And, by the incantations of this verse,

Scatter, as from an unextinguished hearth
Ashes and sparks, my words among mankind!
Be through my lips to unawakened earth

The trumpet of a prophecy! O, Wind,
If Winter comes, can Spring be far behind?

William Blake

London

I wander through each chartered street,
Near where the chartered Thames does flow,
And mark in every face I meet
Marks of weakness, marks of woe.

In every cry of every man,
In every infant's cry of fear,
In every voice, in every ban,
The mind-forged manacles I hear:

How the chimney-sweeper's cry
Every blackening church appalls;
And the hapless soldier's sigh
Runs in blood down Palace walls.

But most, through midnight streets I hear
How the youthful harlot's curse
Blasts the new-born Infant's tear,
And blights with plagues the Marriage-hearse.

William Blake

The Chimney Sweeper

A little black thing in the snow,
Crying “weep! weep!” in notes of woe!
“Where are thy father and mother? Say!”--
“They are both gone up to the church to pray.

“Because I was happy upon the heath,
And smiled among the winter's snow,
They clothed me in the clothes of death,
And taught me to sing the notes of woe.

“And because I am happy and dance and sing,
They think they have done me no injury,
And are gone to praise God and his priest and king,
Who make up a heaven of our misery.”

Lord George G. Byron

Sonnet on Chillon

Eternal Spirit of the chainless Mind!
Brightest in dungeons, Liberty, thou art;
For there thy habitation is the heart -
The heart which love of thee alone can bind;
And when thy sons to fetters are consigned,
- To fetters, and the damp vault's dayless gloom -
Their country conquers with their martyrdom,
And Freedom's fame finds wings on every wind.
Chillon! thy prison is a holy place,
And thy sad floor and altar, for 'twas trod,
Until his very steps have left a trace,
Worn, as if thy cold pavement were a sod,
By Bonnivard. -May none those marks efface!
For they appeal from tyranny to God.

Anna Laetitia Barbauld

The Rights of Women

Yes, injured Woman! rise, assert thy right!
Woman! too long degraded, scorned, opprest;
O born to rule in partial Law's despite,
Resume thy native empire o'er the breast!

Go forth arrayed in panoply divine;
That angel pureness which admits no stain;
Go, bid proud Man his boasted rule resign,
And kiss the golden sceptre of thy reign.

Go, gird thyself with grace; collect thy store
Of bright artillery glancing from afar;
Soft melting tones thy thundering cannon's roar,
Blushes and fears thy magazine of war.

Thy rights are empire: urge no meaner claim,--
Felt, not defined, and if debated, lost;
Like sacred mysteries, which withheld from fame,
Shunning discussion, are revered the most.

Try all that wit and art suggest to bend
Of thy imperial foe the stubborn knee;
Make treacherous Man thy subject, not thy friend;
Thou mayst command, but never canst be free.

Awe the licentious, and restrain the rude;

Soften the sullen, clear the cloudy brow:
Be, more than princes' gifts, thy favors sued;--
She hazards all, who will the least allow.

But hope not, courted idol of mankind,
On this proud eminence secure to stay;
Subduing and subdued, thou soon shalt find
Thy coldness soften, and thy pride give way.

Then, then, abandon each ambitious thought,
Conquest or rule thy heart shall feebly move,
In Nature's school, by her soft maxims taught,
That separate rights are lost in mutual love.

Words & Phrases

aery: (adj) of the air; ethereal.
appall: (v) to fill with dread.
Baiae: (n) an ancient resort city in SW Italy.
Bonnivard: (n) Francois Bonivard (1496-1570), the Genovois monk imprisoned in Chillon that the sonnet is about.
chartered: (adj) a written form granting ownership; owned.
clarion: (n) horn.
consign: (v) to give over the care of one person or thing to another.
dirge: (n) a funeral song.
efface: (v) to erase.
eminence: (n) high station.
fetter: (n) a chain fastened to the feet.
forged: (adj) to be shaped in fire.
hapless: (adj) unlucky.
harlet: (n) a prostitute.
hectic: (adj) excited.
impetuous: (adj) to do rash action.
licentious: sexually unrestrained; lewd.
Maenad: (n) a frantic female follower of Dionysus, the Greek god of wine.
manacle: (n) handcuffs.
maxim: (n) an expression of truth.
oozy: (adj) damp.
panoply: (n) a suit of armor.
pumice: (adj) porous volcanic glass.
sod: (n) grass.

sue: (v) to woo or court.
surge: (n) a strong blast of wind.
Thames: (n) the main river that runs through London.
verge: (n) edge.

Study Questions

1. Shelley's "Ode to the West Wind" is written in *terza rima*, a three line stanza with a strict rhyme scheme. What is the rhyme scheme of this ode? You will notice that the first and third lines rhyme, and that the second line starts the rhyme in the following stanza. This continues throughout the poem. How does the use of *terza rima* add to the images and idea of the poem? How is each stanza connected with the others in terms of metaphors, idea, and sound?

2. What idea in the second stanza of "Ode to the West Wind" connects it with the first? What connects the third stanza with the second?

3. Why is the narrator chained in the fourth stanza of Shelley's ode? Is it similar to the way the "mind-forg'd manacles" in Blake's "London"? Explain.

4. What causes the narrators so much sorrow in both "London" and "The Chimney Sweeper"?

5. Blake talks about "mind-forg'd manacles" in his poem "London." What is the symbolism behind this image?

6. The opening line of Byron's sonnet, "Eternal Spirit of the chainless Mind!" is very powerful. What do you think it means?

7. Byron's "Sonnet on Chillon" is a sonnet. In what ways, though, has it broken the classical conventions of a sonnet?

8. Why does the narrator consider liberty to be "brightest in dungeons"?

9. In Barbauld's poem, what metaphors does she use in the third stanza? Is there a pattern in these metaphors? Explain? Why does she use such a pattern? How does it help her make her point?

10. Barbauld's poem takes a drastic turn in the last stanza. How does it do this and why?

11. Do you see "The Rights of Women" as ironic? Explain. Can it be considered "anti-feminist"? Why or why not. Use examples from the poem to support your answer.

Overview Questions of the Text

1. Now that you have read the poems from the twelve themes, do you feel you know more about poetry? Explain.

2. How would you sum up your experience with these twelve themes?

3. Is there a difference between a poet and one who loves poetry? Why or why not? Can just anybody be a poet? Can you? Explain both your answers.

4. Has poetry changed your perspective on the world in any way? Explain.

5. With the growing use of the Internet, anybody who writes a poem can get it out to the world either in print or online. Does this mass publication of poetry cheapen or demean poetry in anyway? Or does it actually help further the art of poetry? Explain.

6. Do you feel you could create poetry? Why or why not?

7. Pick your favorite poem. Prepare an explanation of what the poem means to you and why it is your favorite.

8. After having read these poems, is your perception of the world opened any more than it was before reading and studying these poems? Why or why not? With this knowledge in mind, try to look upon the world through a poet's eyes; discover what the world of perception is really like.

9. Try writing a poem and share it with the class.

Glossary

Allegory

Hidden symbols or meanings in a story that point to other meanings not directly indicated in the text. T. S. Eliot's *The Waste Land* is full of allegory.

Alliteration

The repetition of consonants within a line.

Initial alliteration : repeats the beginning consonant, as in "**h**aving **h**arrowed **h**ell" (Spenser, *Most Glorious Lord of Life*).

Internal (hidden) Alliteration : repeats the consonants inside words. For example,

With impetuous recoil and ja**rr**ing sound
The infe**r**nal doo**r**s, and on their hinges g**r**ate
Ha**r**sh thunder, that the lowest bottom shook
Of E**r**ebus" (Milton, *Paradise Lost*).

Anapest

A metrical foot that has two short syllables following a long syllable. (See Metrical Foot / Anapestic Foot).

Assonance

Similar to alliteration only that the vowel is repeated either at the beginning or inside the word, as in:

One sh**a**de the more, one r**a**y the less,
Had half impair'd the n**a**meless gr**a**ce
Which w**a**ves in every r**a**ven tress,
Or softly lightens o'er her f**a**ce;

Where th<u>ou</u>ghts serenely sweet expr<u>e</u>ss
How pure, how de**a**r their dw<u>e</u>lling pl**a**ce
(Byron, *She Walks in Beauty*)

Ballad

Traditionally a popular, short folk tale created for the oral tradition, where a scop or Bard would sing, recite, or chant the tale. The "modern" literary ballad has been adapted from this earlier tradition.

Blank Verse

Verse using unrhymed lines using mainly iambic pentameter.

Deep in the shady sadness of a vale
Far sunken from the healthy breath of morn,
Far from the fiery noon, and eve's one star,
Sat gray-haired Saturn, quiet as a stone
(Keats, *Hyperion*).

Caesura

A pause in a line of poetry caused by a punctuation mark of some sort, such as, "She's fickle and false, and there I agree": (Dryden, *Fair Iris I love*).

Catalexis

A line of verse that is missing one or more syllables, mainly in the last foot. Used for accenting syllables for a rhyme. An example is,

Tyger! Tyger! burning bright
In the forests of the night,

What immortal hand or eye
Could frame thy fearful symmetry?
(Blake, *The Tyger!*)

Here, the first three lines have seven syllables, but the final line has eight.

Couplet

A couplet contains two lines in a poem that usually rhyme. For example,

So long as men can breathe, or eyes can see,
So long lives this, and this gives life to thee.
(Shakespeare, *Sonnet XVIII*)

End Rhyme

Where the last syllable of one line rhymes with the last syllable of another. A couplet is but one example of end rhyming. The opposite is an **internal rhyme**.

Feminine Rhyme

Rhymes of two or more syllables stressing any syllable besides the last, such as TURtle, FERtile; Able, CAble; STRAIning, COMPLAIning; SLOWly, HOly.

Of a pool so pitchblack, fell-FROWNing,
It rounds and rounds Despair to DROWNing.
(Hopkins, *Inversnaid*)

Foot

A combination of any stressed or unstressed syllable in a unit of poetic meter. See Metrical Foot.

Internal Rhyme

A rhyme that occurs within the line but does not occur at the end of the line, as in "I bring fresh showers, for the thirsting flowers" (Shelley, *The Cloud*). The opposite is an **End Rhyme**.

Metrical Foot

A meter is a pattern of stressed and unstressed syllables in a poetic line. In English poetry, the number of stresses per line determines meter. The metrical foot is the basic unit of meter. These are the most common metrical feet:

Iambic foot : The most common foot using two syllables of unstressed~STRESSED, as in, " Thou WERE not BORN for DEATH, imMORTal BIRD" (Keats, *Ode to a Nightingale*).

Pyrrhic foot : The most common foot for classical Greek poetry using two syllables of unstressed~unstressed that sit between two regular feet, as in, "MUSE, tell ME of a MAN of MANy WILES" (Homer, *Odyssey*).

Anapestic foot : The least common foot to occur in an entire poem using three syllables of unstressed~unstressed~STRESSED, as in, "Though i SANG in my CHAINS like the SEA" (Thomas, *Fern Hill*).

Trochaic foot : More common in short poems than in longer ones, the trochaic foot uses two syllables of STRESSED~unstressed, as in " LIttle LAMB, who MADE thee? / DOST thou KNOW who MADE thee?" (Blake, *The Lamb*).

Dactylic foot : Uncommon in English verse, the dactylic foot uses three syllables of STRESSED~unstressed~unstressed, as in “KNOW ye the LAND where the CYpress and MYRtle” (Byron, *The Bride of Abydos*).

Free Verse

As the name implies there is considerable freedom from any set rules of rhyme and meter established in classical verse. Yet, there are still various poetical devices available to the poet for poetic variety. T. S. Eliot's The *Wasteland* is a good example of free verse poetry.

Heroic Couplet

Basically, a couplet written in iambic pentameter. Pope's *The Rape of the Lock* employs heroic couplet throughout.

Measure

Poetic rhythm established by the syllables in a line of poetry. The most common forms of measure are:

iamb (unstressed~stressed)
trochee (stressed~unstressed)
anapest (unstressed~unstressed~stressed)
dactyl (stressed~unstressed~unstressed)
Spondee (stressed~ stressed)
pyrrhic (unstressed~unstressed).

Meter

The main metrical foot of the poem combined with the number of feet per line determines the meter. The most common forms of meter are:

Monometer : one foot per line
Dimeter : two feet per line
Trimeter : three feet per line

Tetrameter : four feet per line
Pentameter : five feet per line
Hexameter : six feet per line
Heptameter : seven feet per line
Octameter : eight feet per line

Octave
An eight-line stanza.

Ottava Rima
A stanza of eight lines containing the rhyme scheme of *abababcc.*

Ode
A lengthy lyrical poem using lofty language through formalized stanzas. Odes were originally taken from the Greek, which means "song," but the Greek form of the ode was seldom used in English. Instead two other forms were adapted, the homostrophic ode and the irregular ode.

Homostrophic ode : contains stanzas of the same length and identical rhythm. Shelley's *Ode to the West Wind* and Keat's *Ode on Melancholy* are good examples.
Irregular ode : follows the poets artistic and emotional needs, following neither set rhythm nor length. Coleridge's *Dejection: An Ode* and Wordsworth's *Ode: Intimations of Immortality* are good examples.

Paradox
A statement that appears contrary to common sense or contains contrary elements but when viewed from another angle are essentially true.

Pastorals

Verse that deals with the peaceful and ideal life that shepherds lived.

Pastoral Elegy

a poem that laments the death of a person, but unlike the elegy, in the pastoral elegy, all of nature joins in the lament like in Milton's *Lycidas*.

Satire

A work of literature that depicts through ridicule the corrupt and foolish nature of humanity. The intent of the author is usually as moral criticism aimed at injustice and social error to instruct the reader and society, though many readers and critics perceive it as gross mockery. Swift's *Modest Proposal* is a great example of social satire.

Scansion

The marking of rhythm in a line of poetry to understand its meter (i. e. iambic pentameter) through a scanning process.

Sonnet

a strict fourteen-line poem using the rhyme scheme of iambic pentameter.

Two kinds of sonnets : **Italian sonnet & Shakespearean Sonnet**

Spenserian Stanza

A stanza developed by Spenser for the *Faerie Queene* that has nine lines with the rhyme scheme of *ababbcbcc*. He also developed a stanza of eighteen lines for *Epithalamion* with the same rhyme scheme doubled.

Sprung Rhythm

Rhythm based on the daily speech of ordinary people. Brought to notoriety by Gerard Manley Hopkins, he used feet of various lengths from one to four syllables that could be written with a stressed or a unstressed style of rhythm.

> Oh the MIND, MIND has MOUNtains; CLIFFS of FALL FRIGHTful, SHEER, no-man-FATHomed. HOLD them CHEAP.
>
> (Hopkins, *No Worst, There is None*)

Symbol

An object or representation that implies additional meaning beyond its own.

Terza Rima

Stanzas of three rhyming lines, usually in iambic pentameter, containing the rhyme scheme of *aba, bcb, cdc,* and so on.

Index of First Lines

Index of Authors & Titles

Fifty Recited Poems
Read by Steven Reeder
Recorded at Dongseo University Studio
Edited by Oksun Kang

Contents

23. Emily Dickinson -Because I Could Not Stop For Death
24. John Donne - Death Be Not Proud
25. George Herbert - Death
26. Walt Whitman - O Captain! My Captain!
27. W.B. Yeats - A Coat
28. William Blake - A Poison Tree
29. Stephen Crane - The Heart
30. Claude McKay - America
31. Alexander Pope - Ode on Solitude
32. T.S. Eliot - The Winter Evening Settles Down
33. Thomas Hardy - The Convergence of the Twain
34. Archibald Macleish - Ars Poetica
35. Marianne Moore - Poetry
36. William Wordsworth - Daffodils
37. George Herbert - Easter Wings
38. George Herbert - The Altar
39. Steven Reeder - Uroboros
40. Ezra Pound - In a Station in the Metro
41. Carl Sandburg - Fog
42. William Blake - The Lamb
43. William Blake - The Tyger
44. W.B. Yeats - The Second Coming
45. John Donne - Holy Sonnet 14
46. George Herbert - The Collar
47. William Blake - London
48. William Blake - The Chimney Sweeper
49. George G. Byron - Sonnet on Chillon
50. Anna Laetitia Barbauld - The Rights of Women

저 자 소 개

강옥선 Oksun Kang

부산대학교 박사학위 취득
동서대학교 영어학과 부교수

저 서: *The Close and Holy Darkness: Discovering Western Short Stories* (신아사, 2006), 공저
블레이크와 작은 천국(동인, 2004), 공저
Reading British Poetry (동인, 2004), 공저

논 문: 낭만기 여성시인의 도덕적 감수성 읽기 (2005)
블레이크의 예언시와 사회의식 (2001)

스티븐 리더 Steven Reeder

캘리포니아 주립대학 석사학위 취득
동서대학교 전임강사 (ISP 프로그램)

저 서: *The Close and Holy Darkness: Discovering Western Short Stories* (신아사, 2006), 공저
Reading British Poetry (동인, 2004), 공저

논 문: Dracula as a Tragic Hero: The Illumination of Film on a Text (2006)